21 DAYS TO

Understand

Qabalah

Also in the 21 Days series

Publisher's Note

Research has shown that establishing a habit requires 21 days' practice. That's why Hay House has decided to adapt the work of some of its most prestigious authors into these short, 21-day courses, designed specifically to develop new mastery of subjects such as Qabalah.

Other titles that will help you to explore further the concepts featured in the 21-day program are listed at the beginning of this book.

Introduction

Before we get started, let's get clear that Qabalah is not the same system as Madonna studies—Kabbalah. The main difference seems to be the way the information is ordered and the content differs, although both use very similar language; they come from the same root. For me the "Q," as I affectionately call it, holds true to my astrological and pagan beliefs whilst embracing all New Age laws and systems that seem to have their root in the Tree of Life.

For me the Qabalah is simply a way of studying the worlds we live in—that's no typing error, I do mean the plural "worlds." We are spiritual beings having an earthly experience, but we don't need to lose our spiritual connection in order to do so. The occult adage "As above, so below," encapsulates this perfectly. The simple yet highly complex symbol of the Tree of Life helps us reconnect with our spiritual selves.

The Tree of Life encompasses everything in the Universe among its shapes, circles, and pathways, which are, in fact, symbols of the planets and the Major Arcana of the Tarot. All life's experiences are there: all our emotional trials from joy to pain; all our physical wants and desires; all countries and governments; all angels and astral beings. The Tree of Life holds them all.

Think of it like a map—if you get lost you reach for a map and you find out where you are, where you want to go, and how you're going to get there. Once you learn to read *this* map you can use it to give your life new direction. It will enable you to speed up the journey by taking the right route *for you* instead of being distracted and straying from your path. However, the Tree of Life does *not* and will *never* tell you what to do. The first rule is always *free will*.

Within these pages I present information and techniques I have learned along the way, which I hope will help you to make changes in your life, as I have in mine. In fact, from the very first day I turned up at a class, the Qabalah has been a companion that I trust to help me find my way through the journey of life.

I was fortunate enough to spend over a decade working on the Tree in regular training and I carry on learning from it today. Through this introduction to the Qabalah I sincerely hope you are inspired to start out on your own lifelong journey and enjoy developing your relationship with the Universe that it represents.

From my heart to yours,

David Wells

DAY 1

The Symbolism of the Tree of Life

"The best leaders... almost without exception and at every level, are master users of stories and symbols."
TOM PETERS

The Tree of Life in its very basic form is a symbol, a drawing that holds within it the very essence of the Universe, so today we are going to learn a bit about its symbolism.

Like all symbols, it can't come alive until you breathe life into it. Consider a statue of your favorite spiritual icon, be it Buddha, Christ or Archangel Michael. The plaster, bronze, or even golden statue is itself just a statue, but it's the embodiment, the spiritual energy that's been invested in the image, that makes it so very special to you, to all of us.

For centuries symbols have rallied nations. What is a flag but a symbol? Banners have separated humanity and still do, so you see it's not such a surprise that the Tree of Life symbol holds so much power, considering it has had thousands of years of energy poured into making it so.

Symbols work on our subconscious minds. They bring with them many meanings all wrapped up in one simple drawing, picture, or icon, as well a vibration of their very own— something that will become increasingly important as we go on. Think of a statue of the Buddha. What do you see when you look at it? What do you feel? How does it change you? What do you aspire to when you walk away from it? Does it help you to center yourself and to think of certain symbols? And if it does, do you do that often enough?

Now imagine a symbol that does everything the Buddha statue does but also points out where you are now, what you could do to help yourself if you wish to change, and will also attract into your life the right energy to help you get there. This symbol also holds communication points with your angels, your guides, your Aunty Vera, and your soul, as well as showing you how to deal with co-workers, what your life purpose is, and just why you should avoid wearing red. This symbol is all things to all people—it's the Tree of Life.

Now think about negative symbols, the things that draw you toward dour thoughts rather than positive ones—because they have just as much power. Removing them from your life is important; you do not need them and no matter how they come, it's time to say goodbye to them. Start by switching off the news channel—even the sound of the theme music to the news will prompt negativity because if you watch death, destruction, and argumentative politicians, your head will be full of those thoughts and your downbeat responses will overshadow the lightness of your spirit.

Now I'm not advocating that you live in a world of your own, oblivious to what's going on in the world. It's just that for now I'd like you to concentrate on yourself: your soul, your spirit, and your link with the divine. The truth is by doing this and giving off positive energy, you're helping others without fuelling the energy of those who feed on negativity.

The Tool Kit

Today is also about gathering the things you need for the journey. Look out for them and buy them if you don't already have them. They should be inspiring to you— spiritually inspiring things that lift your spirit, so that when you see them they automatically prepare you for powerful mediations and bring the magic into your life.

- A journal in which you can write down everything you experience, every symbol you see, and every feeling, thought, or sign that comes your way, because it will all be relevant. Also, use it as your dream book to record your dreams during this course, as your subconscious will continue to give you information even when you're asleep.

- A good book or dictionary of symbols, or access to such information on the internet. This is a resource that will help you decipher the meaning of, say, a dove or a rose, or that lion that keeps popping up in visualizations. As you learn the meanings of symbols, you build your own store that your subconscious can use to help keep you on track.

- A pack of Tarot or oracle cards. I use the Thoth Tarot deck. You can take a card daily and use the symbols on the card to positively charge your day, as well as provide you with more information to help you understand the Tree of Life.

- A picture or statue of your favorite spiritual icon, such as Jesus Christ, the Buddha, and so on.

- A candle holder.

- Tealights.

- An incense burner and incense.

- A small bell.

- A beautiful piece of cloth.

Setting Your Intention

What do you want from these 21 days? You can, and probably will, adapt things as you go along, so don't think you're committed to deciding right now. Taking your time to think about what you want gives the Universe a heads up so that it can bring it to you. It's about clarity. Spend some time today thinking about one goal, for now, that you would really like to manifest in your life, and use the next few days to focus on it.

Write that goal in your journal; start it with words "I AM…." Be clear about what you are doing and how you feel when you're doing it, then add the words "open to more of the same or better." Then give yourself a time frame. Again be realistic about it—the Universe does need some time to manifest your desires! Here's an example: "I AM in my new job working with animals and I feel valued, happy, financially rewarded and open to more of the same or better." Take some time out of your day to spend in quiet reflection; a rest before your journey begins, to reconnect yourself to the incredible being you truly are.

Now it's time for your first act to begin to reconnect with your spiritual self.

Perchance to Dream

After some quiet reflection, have a bath, unwind, and relax; be with your own thoughts and, when you're ready, go to bed. As you lie in bed, close your eyes and review the day you've just had. Wind it backward from the moment you got into bed and consider anything you found stressful or thought you could have done differently. Visualize it surrounded with pink light and then let it go—let that bubble of light take it away. Keep winding back your day. If you fall asleep as you do so, don't worry. But if you do make it to the last (first) event—getting up that morning—take a deep breath and release it, then allow yourself to drift off to sleep. You have "cleansed" your day and are ready for tomorrow's adventures!

Tomorrow you will need a sheet of US letter (A4) paper, a coin about 25mm in diameter, a pencil, and a ruler.

DAY 2

Drawing on the Tree of Life

"All religions, arts, and sciences are branches of the same tree. All these aspirations are directed toward ennobling man's life: lifting it from the sphere of mere physical existence and leading the individual toward freedom."

ALBERT EINSTEIN

The first thing you're going to do is to take an oracle or Tarot card. Now write down in your journal what it is and what it means. We will start each day in this way.

To get a better understanding of the Tree of Life and to begin to understand its structure, today I'd like you to draw it (now you know why you needed a coin and ruler for today's session!).

I will explain briefly what you're drawing and why as we go along, but more in-depth explanations will follow later. Like the Tree, you will build your knowledge piece by piece, adding layer upon layer, and filling your symbol bank with riches enough to last many lifetimes.

To help you, here's what you're aiming for.

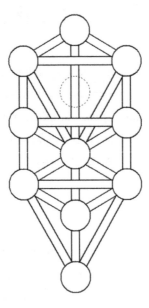

Figure 2.1 A blank Tree of Life

Don't panic, it's not as complicated as it looks! Just take your time and follow one step at a time, and it will all make sense.

You will see that the Tree of Life is made up of ten interconnected circles. A circle or sphere in the Tree of Life is called a Sephira (the plural is Sephiroth). See them as powerhouses of energy. They are states of being, not necessarily destinations, and they will show themselves as conditions in your life and in the lives of those around you.

So let's begin. Take a blank sheet of US letter (A4) paper, find the center vertically, and draw a faint pencil line from top to bottom. Now find the midpoint between that line and the edge of the paper on both the right- and left-hand sides, and mark them. This gives you three lines on which to center your circles, known as the Spheres, and balance your Tree.

Now take your coin and place it at the top of your paper, center it on your middle line and draw around it. This circle is Kether, number one, where it all begins. Write the word "Kether" inside the circle and put the number one in there as well. Kether is where the divine in us and in the Universe sits, paused waiting for the manifestation process to begin, holding onto every creative idea there is and ever will be until it's accessed.

Next drop down to your right-hand side and draw another circle. Write the word "Chokmah" (pronounced "hok-ma" with the "ch" making a sound like the "ch" in the Scottish word "loch") and the number two. Here those creative ideas are stimulated, charged with energy, and hooked into the grid.

Move across to the left-hand side of your page on the same level as Chokmah and draw your next circle. This is number three and it's called Binah ("bee-na"). It's here that those ideas and the energy we've mentioned are first given form, structure, and direction.

Now move back to the right-hand side under Chokmah and draw circle number four, Chesed ("hes-ed"). As you do so, consider what excites you in life, what opportunities come when ideas flow, and how you can sometimes get carried away with it all.

Then it's back to the left for the next circle, which is number five and called Geburah ("ge-boo-rah"). This represents making changes and cutting away excess, and the realization that some things aren't necessary or even desirable.

Into the center now as you draw Tiphareth ("tiff-a-reth") and number six. If you look at this circle you will see it sits in the center of the Tree. It's all about balance and finding the beauty in the moment.

Back to the right and the next circle, Netzach ("net-sack"). This is number seven and where you acknowledge your feelings. For the first time in this journey things get personal and seem to relate directly to day-to-day stuff.

Then over to the left to draw Hod, number eight. Your thoughts and images are represented here. Whether they are negative or positive, you have the power to change your attitude simply by changing your mind, no matter what's going on around you.

Then it's back to the center and Yesod, number nine. Here is where you store all your emotions, your memories, and your past-life conditioning, which can result in you getting lost in repeating cycles.

Finally you come to the last circle, Malkuth ("mal-kooth"), number ten. Take a look around you for here you are, on Earth, as you are currently living, in Malkuth. The question to ponder: Is this the end point or the beginning?

As you look at the Tree before you add the next stage, the paths, what are simply ten circles on a page will have begun to make more sense. By attaching words to the symbols you have drawn, you start to imbue them with their magical energy, and that in turn brings the attention of Universal energies your way as they recognize the efforts you're making and the light you're switching on.

Today we have worked on the basic symbol and tomorrow, after we have drawn in the paths and looked at more shapes that help explain the relationships between the Sephiroth, you will be able to check that your Tree of Life is accurate by comparing it with Figure 3.1 (see Day 3).

Lightning Flash

If you look back at you the order in which you drew the Sephiroth, you will notice that it follows a pattern, which directs the energy in a certain way:

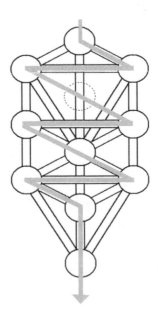

Figure 2.2 Energy pattern through the Sephiroth

If you follow the energy through, you can begin to see how the process of manifestation works.

- Kether—an idea is waiting to be recognized and grabbed.

- Chokmah—it's charged with the spark of creativity.

- Binah—structure is put around it and it's given form.

- Chesed—excitement builds, ideas flow, opportunities exist.

- Geburah—anything unnecessary is removed.

- Tiphareth—balance and the true beauty of the idea shines.

- Netzach—time to invest your feelings and joy into it.

- Hod—time to brand and create the image.

- Yesod—remember old pitfalls and learn from the past.

- Malkuth—time to bring the idea to fruition, to land it here on Earth.

This process of manifestation works for your soul's incarnation right through to the batch of cupcakes you've made. The more you know about it, the more you can take control of the process, so you can get that recipe just right.

Da'ath

You will have noticed that on the above diagram, between Binah and Chokmah, and just below Kether, there is a dotted circle. This is called Da'ath, the Great Abyss, and for the purposes of this introduction we won't be looking into it! It's a point that's a little too advanced for this 21-day course to cover, but it's good to know that it's there. In short, it's about faith, taking a leap, and being so sure of yourself and your link to the spiritual worlds that nothing—no-thing— can sway you.

Tonight, I'd like you to consider the goal you thought of earlier—to think about your dream, and how it might manifest using the Tree. In your head go through each step, from the idea to landing it here on Earth, and know that dreams do come true. All the time.

DAY 3

The Tarot Paths

*"You cannot travel the path until you
have become the path itself."*

THE BUDDHA

**Pick an oracle or Tarot card, and in your journal
write down what card it is and what it means.**

Today you're going to return to your drawing of the Tree
because all those circles now need to be linked by a network
of paths. Each path has a specific meaning and, as part of your
journey, the paths will have a specific experience attached
to them.

Refer back to Figure 2.1 and, using your ruler, draw in the paths that connect the Sephiroth now. For the moment, leave them blank—we will discuss their meanings in a moment.

When you've done that, look at the next drawing. Check that what you've done so far on your own Tree is accurate. Now notice the names on the paths.

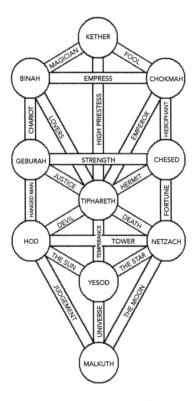

Figure 3.1 Annotated Tree of Life

Anyone familiar with the Tarot will know that these paths represent the 22 Major Arcana cards of the Tarot deck. Each path is named after one of the archetypes or symbols. As you would expect, they draw to you the experience of the card in question, just as meditating on the Tarot card would do, so that you know where you are, what you need to do next, and why you would choose to walk that path.

(I should point out that sometimes the Sephiroth are referred to as paths, too. However, personally I usually distinguish between the two as I feel the Sephiroth are more powerhouses that push energy along the path and they hold a different sort of magic, which you will discover later on.)

If you read the Tarot, think about the names of the paths as you draw the links between the Sephiroth; if you don't read the Tarot, don't worry—the paths will become your teachers as the Tree of Life becomes your guide.

In some decks the Major Arcana have different names. For example, in my own favorite, the Thoth deck, the following names are used: Judgment is Aeon; Temperance is Art; Justice is Adjustment; Strength is Lust. Don't be confused by this, as they hold the same qualities and share symbols. Just go with what's on your own Tarot deck. If you don't have one, let yourself be guided to one. Lose the thought that someone has to buy you one or it has to magically appear from thin air. Go get a deck. Buy one you feel drawn to and when you've got it, meditate with it around you. Let the cards dance in your aura and charge them with your energy.

Complete?

You may be thinking that your Tree is now complete, but far from it! There's so much more to discover. However, you've certainly done enough for today, as you have immersed yourself in its energy for some time while you've drawn and filled in the paths, contemplating them as you went.

Remember, contemplation is like meditation but you're able to eat a cookie whilst you're doing it! It's just as effective a way to contact your inner self and listen to your guides as sitting cross-legged on the floor; it's simply a way of stilling yourself through action. You do the same when you're walking the dog, doing the housework, or even while driving your car. The only difference here is that you lose yourself with your ruler and pencil as you contemplate an ancient symbol that charges you with amazing energy.

Housekeeping

The rest of today is about making sure you're ready for the next part of your journey. Be good to yourself: nurture yourself, drink lots of water and eat great food, and celebrate yourself.

Things are going to get pretty busy as you draw the Tree into your life, so begin by having a tidy-up at home. You might wonder what that has to do with your spiritual advancement, but consider how much you can really concentrate if you know there are dirty dishes in the sink or piles of ironing waiting to be done. And we all know that de-cluttering is good for the soul!

It's up to you what you do, but it's a great idea to tackle something that's been on your mind for ages—maybe the garage needs a good clear-out or perhaps it's time you went through your closet and thinned out all the clothes you no longer wear.

As you carry out this task today, think about what it represents for you. What are you saying by this symbolic action in your life? You're suggesting to your own subconscious that it's time for a change and you're starting by getting rid of the things you no longer need in your life. You're organizing yourself, providing yourself with strong and clear foundations for the task ahead.

When you've done your task, light a candle, burn some incense, and put on some uplifting music. Have a bath if you like. Now notice the energy in the house—how does it feel? Look again at your drawing of the Tree of Life. In fact, put it somewhere you can see it as you go about your daily business now that you've got more of an understanding of how it works. Magic is entering your life—you can sense it by looking the Tree, feeling the change in your energy, and the symbolic act of lighting a candle to bring light into your life.

Tomorrow we'll work further on the Tree, dividing it up some more into some very important and supportive shapes.

DAY 4

Supporting Roles

"Seeing much, suffering much, and studying much are the three pillars of learning."

BENJAMIN DISRAELI

Pick an oracle or Tarot card, and in your journal write down what card it is and what it means.

Yesterday you filled in the paths on your Tree, so today we're going to consider other structures that help bring the Tree to life. First up are the pillars, which are easy to see when you look at your drawing. The one on the left contains Binah, Geburha, and Hod; the central column holds Kether, Tiphareth, Yesod, and Malkuth; and the one on the right encompasses Chokmah, Chesed, and Netzach.

There's no need to draw them on your Tree this time—you can download the diagram from www.davidwells.co.uk if you prefer.

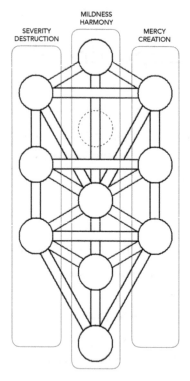

Figure 4.1 The pillars of the Tree of Life

Now let's consider the first pillar, comprising Binah, Geburha, and Hod: the Pillar of Severity.

The Pillar of Severity

Binah

This represents the feminine—you might think it's odd to find this at the top of the Pillar of Severity, but if you think of the decisions a mother must make and how tough love can be, it makes sense. Binah is the Great Mother, directing with an understanding that goes beyond what might be obvious to those who are at the receiving end of such decisions. She shows where you might experience limits, but limits that will ultimately shape your destiny.

Geburah

Often Geburah is seen as challenging, but all it really wants to do is cut away what is no longer required. Sometimes its influence is seen through trials and tribulations, but if you can recognize them as such, you are better equipped to deal with them. This turns what you may have perceived as a weakness into a strength.

Hod

Hod symbolizes worldly matters, such as business and your career, as well as how you approach these things. They are by their very nature analytical. Hod is also how you communicate and what images you create—here sits the very powerhouse of affirmations, as you seek to create your world through positive thoughts and images. It asks, "How do you think?" with your head, your heart, your gut.

The Pillar of Mercy

Chokmah

The opposite number to the Great Mother, Chokmah heads the right-hand pillar and symbolizes the cosmic Father, representing balanced behavior and responsibilities. Logic is the way of Chokmah, but don't think of this as a dull Sephira—it is far from it. When you need to make choices that require both logic and sudden illumination, this is the place to be.

Chesed

Here you're rewarded for the work you put in, the opportunities you are prepared to take, and the adventurous side of your nature that helps you take them. Compassion, peace, and positivity are reflected in Chesed, which helps you to manifest abundance, whether financial or emotional wealth, in your life.

Netzach

Your emotional attachments and feelings are represented here—what you desire and perhaps who you find attractive, as well as who your best friend is and what makes them that. Use Netzach to understand your relationships, what you want from them, and how others make you feel when you're around them.

The Middle Pillar

Kether

At the crown of the Tree of Life, in the middle column, sits your full potential, new starts, and inspirational ideas. Here are the spiritual realms and that place you go to when you're sitting on your rug, eyes closed, at peace with the world. It can also represent where you may lose yourself, if you become so "heavenly minded" that you're no earthly good.

Tiphareth

A beautiful Sephira, Tiphareth represents your higher self or soul. It's all about high ideals as well as where you meet the part of you that would sacrifice everything for those you love. It occupies the center of the Tree and, as such, sits at the center of ourselves and governs balance. Can you remember the last time you felt truly balanced?

Yesod

Habits and cycles are shown here. When you know how to look into the mirror of this Sephira, you will be able to see where particular habits or patterns of behavior come from— this life, past lives…? It also shines a light on your hopes and fears, as well as affecting your physical dreams by allowing the subconscious to communicate clearly, if you want to listen.

Malkuth

Your kingdom on Earth, this is where you live, and in this physical world all that's manifest in your life sits here. Here you become consciously aware of everything above you, to your left and to your right. All you have done gathers in Malkuth, including your physical body, the vehicle for all your thoughts, feelings, dreams, aspirations, logical decisions, adventures, tough love, images and so on.

The Three Pillars Summarized

Severity

The principles of taking tough decisions when they need to be taken, in a way that is firm but fair; what needs to be done in order to move forward to your goal; Divine justice.

Mercy

Your benevolent side; the part of you that wants peace, and when you have found peace, enjoys all the rewards for your efforts; Divine mercy.

Middle

When you have cut away what doesn't work and embraced all the opportunities that have come your way, you find yourself here in a place of balance; Divine equilibrium.

Which End Is Up Again?

Some folks get a little confused as to how to use the Tree in situations that are very personal or perhaps relate to the environment. It's all a question of perspective.

If you are looking at the Tree square on, as you do from the pages of this book, you are looking at the universal Tree—a Tree that's about the world(s) you live in and how that environment affects you.

However, if you imagine sitting with the Tree behind you, with the middle pillar against your spine, this is your personal Tree. (Yes, that does mean that what's on your right as you look at the Tree now, changes to being on your left as you sit with it at your back.)

This is a fundamental rule for working with the Tree: if it's a universal matter, you face the Tree, but if it's a personal issue, you put your spine against the Tree.

Although we are touching on it here, later on you will begin to see how the Tree is building on you physically. The truth is it was always there, but what you're doing now is bringing it to the fore and you will start to feel it in your physical body. Don't believe me? You'll see.

For today we'll leave it there. You have lots to think about, but do relax—the images will do the work as much as the words. Have a cookie and a cup of tea or coffee, then ponder, wonder. For the rest of the day just be the magnificently complex yet oh-so-simple being that you are.

DAY 5

Meeting the Elementals

"Move swift as the Wind and closely-formed as the Wood. Attack like the Fire and be still as the Mountain."

SUN TZU

Pick an oracle or Tarot card, and in your journal write down what card it is and what it means.

Today we are going to take a close look at the elements and their relationship with the Tree of Life. So, which one are you? Are you fire, earth, air, or water? How would you know? Many people think of themselves in terms of the element associated with their astrological sign:

FIRE	EARTH	AIR	WATER
Aries	Taurus	Gemini	Cancer
Leo	Virgo	Libra	Scorpio
Sagittarius	Capricorn	Aquarius	Pisces

Here, then, is the first mention of astrology connected to the Tree of Life, something that's important. We will look at this in more depth later, but don't worry if you know nothing about astrology as yet—you will very soon. One of the joys of the Tree is that it introduces new things, in a way that makes them easy to assimilate, as it grows on you.

So, which sign are you? Write down what element your Sun (also known as Star) sign suggests that you are. If you have studied astrology, look also at your rising sign as well as your Moon sign. These three things can be found very easily: you can put your time and date of birth into a search engine online and find them quickly. (It doesn't matter if you don't know what time you were born, you can still find your Sun and Moon signs.) Once you have discovered what element you are according to your Sun sign, see how it describes you.

The Elements and the Tarot

And just to add something else into today's mix, these elements are also present in the Tarot:

- Fire is Wands.

- Earth is Disks.

- Air is Swords.

- Water is Cups.

If you do read the Tarot you will already know this; if you don't, it's a great way of helping you understand the cards and what they may tell you if you use them in conjunction with the Tree of Life. For example, if you get a lot of Cups when you read the cards, the element of water is dominant. So what does that mean? You're about to find out!

From your deck of Tarot cards, take out the Ace of Wands and look at the fiery nature of the card. As we go along you will need all the aces, which are connected to Kether, number one. But for our purposes now, we're going to examine the elements in their purest form. Purity is Kether. Elements are in your card—already you're working with the Qabalah!

Elemental Correspondences

Now it's time to explore the elements as forces, rather than as something more tangible, such as the heat of the Sun, mountains, rivers, and wind, although they are one and the same.

Fire is perhaps the most ancient symbol of divinity. It is a living principle of duality, providing light and heat to aid humankind, while at the same time being a force of death and destruction. The ancients believed that fire could lie hidden in a piece of wood. By rubbing two pieces together they could often coax the fire from the wood. It's also present in you when you get "fired" up by a creative project or angry with someone who isn't listening and, of course, anytime you like the look of that guy from Accounts, it's fire in the form of desire that's pushing you to ask him out. Fire is connected with Wands in the Tarot, and the astrological signs Aries, Leo, and Sagittarius.

Earth is the element of form, binding, and manifestation. The element of earth is the lowest in vibratory rate of the four elements—you're standing on it. It's practical and steady, it supports and allows for growth, it's about health, wealth, and well-being. When someone is very earthy they are sometimes also described as being stubborn, immovable, or perhaps caught up in making money at the expense of everything and everyone one around them. Earth is also about food and cuddles—we just can't do without it! Earth is linked with Disks in the Tarot, and the astrological signs Taurus, Virgo, and Capricorn.

Air is commonly associated with mental activity, communication, and chatting. It's the element that governs the thought patterns you produce and the images you create in life. We have all heard how every thought becomes a thing—and that thing can be carried in the wind. Someone who is very talkative, perhaps even a gossip, could be said to be as very oriented toward air. But an "airy-fairy person" is altogether different, as they tend to live in their head and do not come down to earth too often, and practical matters are not their strength. Air is connected with Swords in the Tarot, and the astrological signs Gemini, Libra, and Aquarius.

Water is an element associated with the emotions. Think about the tears that come when we get emotional. It's also deceptively strong, as water always wins—even against rock, it will gently carve its way through to get to its destination. Water and your emotions are very powerful forces. When you listen to your emotions, they can guide you using water's biggest tool—your intuition. This is the land of your subconscious mind. Water is linked with Cups in the Tarot, and the astrological signs Cancer, Scorpio, and Pisces.

Take a moment to think of your Sun sign, and those of your close family and friends. Do you know a Gemini who is very airy? Or perhaps a fiery Aries or an earthy Taurus? How about an emotional Cancer? Now think of your elemental traits. Are you an earthy nurturer, who has a hundred plants around the house? Or are you an airy intellectual who likes to read and read and not bother with the washing up so much? Or then again, are you a watery-type who acts on intuition and always gets to where they want to be? Or maybe you have some great ideas but you never take action, because you can't translate the fire and passion of the idea into something practical? Examining your traits in terms of the elements can be very illuminating.

Elemental Beings

To help bring form and symbolism to the elements in the Qabalah, each element has an elemental being associated with it. Some would say these are real—they are to me—whereas others consider them to be just another tool with which to understand the elements. I would agree with that, too. You can make up your own mind.

Fire has the Salamanders, which are not lizards or a type of hot kitchen grill, but little sparks of light that glow red-hot. They also have a king and he is called Djin. He is a bigger version of them and you may see this amazing creature in Day 7's visualization.

Earth has the Gnomes (but not a fishing rod in sight!). These are gnarled, ancient creatures, who work very hard at keeping systems running and Mother Earth tidy—not an easy task these days. Their king is Ghobe, who is bigger in stature than his subjects and is a bit scary, but as long as you don't drop litter and love the Earth, he's benevolent.

Air has the most high-profile elementals, in the form of fairy folk known as Sylphs. They buzz about in the wind bringing thoughts that seem to come out of nowhere your way. When they whisper it's good to listen. Their King is called Paralda, and he appears as a billowing cloud of ever-changing shape and size that asks you to stay a while and chat.

Water has the Undines, who are hard to figure out as they are but sparkles on the water or the shimmer on a lake. Their King is Nixsa, a giant wave that can be all-consuming just as a giant wave of emotion can take over and almost make it impossible for you to function. Nixsa asks that you let him and his Undines help you understand where that emotion is coming from, and what to do with it.

Find an Elemental Place

Today's task is a deceptively simple one. Find yourself a place in nature—for example, sit by a river or a lake, take a walk by the beach or in the park. You can skip through a forest wearing a white cheesecloth skirt and a big hat if you like, but get out in among the elemental kingdoms!

If you can, sit somewhere beautiful. Close your eyes and feel the wind in your hair, the sun on your skin, the earth beneath your feet, and listen to any nearby water. Know that you're connected to all of it, you truly are.

Then write down how you feel about the elements and the elementals, and how they are reflected in you. Are you predominantly fiery, emotional, practical, or talkative? See if you can analyze which elements dominate your personality.

Tomorrow you will start your journey up the Tree of Life.

DAY 6

The Sephiroth: Malkuth

"There is noting on earth you cannot have—once you have mentally accepted the fact that you can have it."
Robert Collie

Pick an oracle or Tarot card, and in your journal write down what card it is and what it means.

Transforming knowledge into experience is what today is all about, through a system that will help you understand each Sephira, and build it into your aura as well as your subconscious.

You're going to start with Malkuth, which is perhaps the obvious place to begin as it represents where you are currently living, and the system that works for Malkuth works for every one of the Sephiroth as well as the 22 paths.

Starting with something called the "correspondences" of the Sephira/Path, these are symbols that represent the energy of the Malkuth Sephira.

- Malkuth: The Kingdom.

- Position on the Tree: Ten, at the bottom of the Middle Pillar.

- Planet: Earth.

- Archangel: Sandalphon.

- Virtue: Discrimination.

- Vices: Greed; inertia.

- Colors: Red, yellow, green, and blue.

- Incense: Dittany of Crete.

- Body parts: The feet; the anus.

- Tarot cards: The four 10s.

This is by no means all of Malkuth's correspondences, but for now it's about simplifying the Tree and helping you understand the process. The most notable new information in this list is the introduction of an Archangel and the Virtue and Vices.

The angelic forces on the Tree are made up of ten great Archangels. They will be listed for you later, but as you move up the Tree the first one you meet, and the last on the way back, is always Sandalphon.

The Archangel of Humanity, Sandalphon sits in Malkuth here on Earth to guide and protect us. For me that last part is very, very important. No journey on the Tree should be undertaken without Sandalphon's blessing. I always check in with him and he usually offers his blessing by touching my head or shoulder before I embark upon another adventure.

The Vice and Virtue of a Sephira offer a very quick reminder of what it's all about. Here the Vice is inertia and the Virtue is discrimination. This simply means that if you do nothing, nothing is what you will get in return. And in a physical world, isn't that the truth! Discrimination means prioritizing what needs to be done next for you to get to where you want to be. So you can see that you probably do both of these every day of your life, which should come as no surprise, as you live on Earth. But what would happen if you did less of the Vice and more of the Virtue?

Terminus

In the great bus journey of manifestation, this is the bit where everything gets off—where all those emotional, spiritual and argumentative thoughts, feelings, ideas, relationships, and so on, will manifest in your life. It's so much more than what you can touch, hear, see, feel, and smell—it's everything that makes you who you are.

But don't be mistaken. As solid as this Sephira feels, it's also open to change, and when you take charge of it you can form it the way you want it to be formed, through action here on Earth as well as action on the spiritual and emotional planes. The thing about Malkuth is it takes time for it all to settle, for bits to be put into place and, no matter how great you are at manifesting things, I can assure you they won't pop up instantly through the floor, no matter how hard you try.

That's the thing about being here on Earth. It is sometimes a challenge, and Malkuth and the Tree recognize that. They are here to help you succeed in a place that to your spiritual self is made of dense energy; where we have to build things physically rather than simply thinking to manifest them. Here on Earth we have to think it, create it, build it.

Look at the four tens in your Tarot deck: what do those images tell you? Ten is the end of a cycle. For today think about what you want here on Earth. Where do you have to stop dithering and take action? What order will you prioritize things in? What's most important and what can wait? And just how do you use the resources you have at your disposal? Could you exchange money for time—get a cleaner, for example? Or maybe you could do the opposite and change some of your time for money? It's all about exchanges of energy.

Look at how you've been over the past few days. Have you started to tidy up, organizing yourself a little better, and maybe saying no to those who leach your time? Are you thinking about money and how to make it work better for you? (Money is very much a Malkuth energy.) Or are you wondering how to attract it into your life by taking action rather than leaving your great ideas loitering around in Hod, waiting for you to get round to them?

The Tree is starting to work.

DAY 7

Malkuth in More Depth

"The best and safest thing is to keep a balance in your life, acknowledge the great powers around us and in us. If you can do that, and live that way, you are really a wise man."

EURIPIDES

Pick an oracle or Tarot card, and in your journal write down what card it is and what it means.

After yesterday's introduction to Malkuth, and now that your foot is on the first step, it seems only fitting that you should see the Tree of Life in all its glory, meet the elementals, and begin to feel their energy within and around you. These are our topics for today.

We are going to start with a visualization. This is something that's a very personal thing, as no two people visualize the same way—you're taking an inward journey that feels as if you're going outside of your consciousness. In short, you're actually doing both as you mix your own energy with universal energy. You become more connected to a greater consciousness.

This visualization is best recorded and played back. Or you can have someone read it to you slowly and gently, allowing yourself time to assimilate the information. If neither is possible, simply read and re-read it until you have the images in your mind, then go for it! Don't worry if you miss something. As long as you have the core message, your visualization will have the desired effect.

It's about seeing the Tree as well as seeing which of the elementals are more prevalent for you—it might be a surprise—and once you see which of the elementals is greatest and which are underrepresented, they will move around to balance your energy. This has the effect of making you feel more balanced, at peace, and connected to—as well as aware of—your own energy. You can do this whenever you feel the need.

Setting Up

There's a very big difference between setting up for a visualization and a full path-working. We will deal with the latter later, in Day 21, but for now simple techniques will help you get the most from this process.

You will also be working with the Qabalistic Cross to help protect your energy and empower your visualizations. Take a moment to read through the set-up; it's very simple.

- Eat about an hour or two beforehand so you're not starving or bloated.

- Switch off all your phones.

- Find a comfortable spot to sit; don't lie down as you might sleep.

- Let everyone know you mustn't be disturbed.

- Light a candle before you begin, with the intention of having a great experience and connecting to your elementals.

- Take a moment to breathe in, nice and deep, for four seconds. Hold it for two, breathe out for four seconds, then hold it for two again. Repeat a few times, each time relaxing more and more.

- Have no expectations; approach each visualization like a child on an adventure.

How to Perform the Qabalistic Cross

Begin the ritual facing east.

- Touch your forehead and vibrate (say out loud) "Ateh" ("a-tay").

- Point toward your feet and "touch" your groin. Vibrate "Malkuth."

- Touch your right shoulder and vibrate "Ve-Geburah" ("vay ge-boo-ra").

- Touch your left shoulder and vibrate "Ve-Gedulah" ("vay ge-doo-la").

- Place your hands together over your heart and vibrate "Le-Olahm" ("lay oo-lam").

- Finish by saying "Amen."

This simply means "As above, so below; the power and the glory; for ever and ever, Amen," but it pre–dates Christianity by many thousands of years. It's the vibration of the words that makes the difference, so really give it some oomph!

Once you're comfortable, you've lit your candle, and switched off your phone, begin by breathing. Close your eyes and let go of those stresses and strains.

Visualization: The Tree of Life and the Elementals

Now it's time to begin the visualization.

See yourself in a forest. Build it around you and make it as real as you can. See it, feel it, hear it, and smell it. Walk along the path and if an animal comes your way, acknowledge it. This is another symbol—an aspect of yourself or perhaps a power animal just for you.

Follow the path to a clearing, a well-kept place with flower borders and a beautiful lawn. At the far end you see a giant oak tree. It's magnificent! It has an aura around it that sparkles in the light and it seems to vibrate in a magical way. It's the Tree of Life. Stop and feel its magic.

In its base is a great oak door that opens as you approach. Step inside. At first you notice the smell of damp earth and wood.

Then the aroma of herbs fills your nostrils as you move into this space—the Temple of Malkuth.

You look down and see herbs strewn across a black-and-white tiled floor. They release their fragrance as you walk over them. Your eyes become accustomed to the light and you begin to peer around you. The walls are covered in oak and ahead of you there is a double-cubed altar, with one cube of ebony and one of ivory. On the altar there is a simple white cloth with a blue crystal bowl set upon it. In the bowl burns a flame. Ahead of the altar are two pillars, one of ebony and one of ivory. Behind them are three great doors.

On the eastern wall above the three great doors is a circular stained-glass window featuring the face of a man, which represents Aquarius and the symbol for Air. To your right and in the south there is another window, showing a lion rampant (a lion in an upright position, as seen on the Scottish flag). This is the symbol for Leo and Fire. Behind you in the west, the window depicts an eagle flying into a golden sun—the symbol for Scorpio and Water. And to your left, in the north, the window shows a black bull in a field of poppies—the symbol for Taurus and Earth.

Stand in the center of the temple and await the presence of Archangel Sandalphon. As he appears, the atmosphere changes. This humble and magnificent being comes toward you, his robe the colors of earth: red, olive, and brown. These robes seem to weigh him down for he is the Archangel of Humanity, charged with our care. He smiles and welcomes you, and asks you to face the eastern wall. He then places his hand on your shoulder or head in a blessing. As he steps back he raises his hands and claps them.

From the eastern wall comes Paralda, a great billowing cloud of air and with him the sylphs. Next, from the southern wall comes Djin, a wall of fire with coal-black eyes, and with him the salamanders. From the western wall comes a crashing wave of water—Nixsa and his Undines. And from the northern walls struts Ghobe, his legions of gnomes marching with order and purpose. All the elementals stand, each waiting for their king's signal.

The elemental kings step aside and reveal how much Air, Fire, Water, and Earth you currently have. What do you see? Are you busy with Water, empty of Fire? How are you made up right now?

The elementals begin to move toward you. Don't be frightened. They dance around you, balancing you. They help you find enthusiasm where Fire might be lacking; to speak out where more Air is needed; to be more practical and ordered where Earth is in need of cultivation; or let go to express a wave of emotion when Water is required.

Soon they retreat, leaving you standing in the middle of the temple. Take a moment to reflect, to feel this peace and balance, to notice any ideas that are now flooding into your mind as enthusiasm replaces apathy, solutions replace questions, and action calls where inertia held you back.

Sandalphon appears, smiling, and embraces you. He guides you out of the temple and as you leave, the oak tree the door closes. You don't feel sad—you can come back whenever you need to.

You (and your animal, if you've seen one) return to the clearing and then go back into the forest. You say farewell to the animal and let the forest fade as you bring yourself back into the here and now.

Slowly open your eyes, and wiggle your fingers and your toes. If you wish, you can now get up, make yourself a hot drink and have a cookie or two.

Recording Your Journey

Once you're refreshed, get out your journal and a pen. Before you switch your phone back on, make yourself comfortable and write out your experience. Here are some prompts to help you.

- Think about everything you've seen; if you had an animal, what does the kind of animal you saw tell you?

- How did the Tree make you feel?

- How did Sandalphon make you feel?

- Which of the elementals was greater, which not so much?

- What happened when they balanced you out?

- Can you hang on to that feeling?

- What ideas and solutions have come to you—practical steps to help you in your life in the here and now?

- What is your plan of action?

- What can you do today to get things underway?

Once you have consolidated your visualization, you might find that opportunities to start putting your ideas into action come your way. You need to grasp these as, magical as the Tree is, it can't do it all for you. So take the opportunities and be ready for the next adventure to show up in your life. Remember, the Tree will manifest both opportunities and challenges. It will bring all of each Sephiroth's experiences your way, and by taking action you can bring that goal you identified at the beginning of this process into manifestation.

Well done and welcome to Malkuth!

DAY 8

The Planetary Influences

"Man is a microcosm, or a little world, because he is an extract from all the stars and the planets of the whole firmament, from the earth and the elements; and so he is their quintessence."

<small>PHILIPUS AUREOLUS PARACELSUS</small>

Pick an oracle or Tarot card, and in your journal write down what card it is and what it means.

To help you with today's session, please have a blank Tree of Life to hand. There is one on the Qabalah drop-down menu on my web page www.davidwells.co.uk that you can download and print. If any of this is problematic, use the one you've already drawn.

Today we are exploring the planetary influences on the Tree of Life. Each of the Sephiroth is associated with a planet. This helps us to understand the force, but it also opens up the world of astrology to the student of the Qabalah—and a little astrological knowledge goes a long way. If you already study astrology, I'd still like you to do this exercise, because you will see how the planets influence their relevant Sephira, which will help build even more symbolism into the memory banks in your subconscious. I have also added a color for each Sephira.

So, let's begin.

♆ Kether	♅ Chokmah	♄ Binah	♃ Chesed	♂ Geburah
☉ Tiphareth	♀ Netzach	☿ Hod	☽ Yesod	⊗ Malkuth

Kether: Number one; planet Neptune

Draw the symbol for Neptune, which looks like a trident, on your Tree in the relevant position—where Kether stands. Neptune is the planet of mystery; it's veiled and sometimes hard to see behind. It governs magic and all things mystical. It is fitting, then, that it sits at the top of the Tree of Life. Leave the circle white.

Chokmah: Number two; planet Uranus

Now put the symbol for Uranus where Chokmah sits—it resembles a TV aerial. The electric force that comes from this planet and is shown in the Sephira gives energy to your ideas, inspiring and putting the spark of life into the Tree. It takes nothing and turns it into something. Color this Sephira gray.

Binah: Number three; planet Saturn

Saturn with his rings around him brings form to the Tree, and here in Binah the first rules are applied. By acknowledging the laws of the Universe, all things come into manifestation. Saturn brings order soon enough where it is lacking. Put Saturn's perfect form on your Tree. Shade this one black.

Chesed: Number four; planet Jupiter

The symbol for Jupiter is easy to remember as it looks like a number four. Jupiter is benevolent; he's the gift-giver who offers abundance. But sometimes abundance is in itself hard to deal with, as it can lead to excess. This Sephira is where we get carried away with adventure, and Jupiter has a big smile, large pockets, and a generous nature. Draw him on your Tree and color the circle blue.

Geburah: Number five; planet Mars

As this symbol is often used to signify "male", you won't be surprised to learn that Mars is the planet that governs war, anger, passion, and football. In Geburah we examine what has to go; what confrontation has to happen so that things can run smoothly; what lessons need to be learned and delivered. Mars cuts away what's no longer required. Put him in and color him red.

Tiphareth: Number six; planet the Sun

A circle with a dot in the center, the Sun is our life force and the balancing point on the Tree—the place where the Tree can be reflected horizontally as well as vertically. This planet is one of healing. It makes us all feel good when we feel its energy upon us and it lights our way. Its color is sometimes seen as gold, but yellow will do just fine.

Netzach: Number seven; planet Venus

This is the symbol for "female" and, of course, Venus is a goddess. She represents feminine energy, love, and feelings, as well as everything to do with nature. Often seen looking fabulous, wearing white, surrounded by animals, and generally being adored, she brings her grace and charm to the position of Netzach. Color her green—what else would she be?

Hod: Number eight; planet Mercury

The talkative one, Mercury is the winged god of communication. This is the planet of images and it sits perfectly in Hod, where you can create your own pictures before you manifest your dreams and goals. This boy is fleet of foot and can occasionally cause mischief, as we sometimes inadvertently visualize things we don't really want, sometimes through fear and sometimes through the power of advertising that encourages us to buy stuff we don't really need. Be aware of this aspect of Hod. Color him orange.

Yesod: Number nine; planet the Moon

Please always draw Yesod in this way, as it symbolizes a "happy" Moon, one that is waxing, gaining power instead of losing it. The Moon is about your emotions, which are distinct from your feelings. She is silvery, like a mirror, and holds more information in your subconscious than you will ever have time to use! Past life work is often associated with

Yesod and the Moon's influence stands behind many of your reactions. Color Yesod silver and violet.

Malkuth: Number ten; planet Earth

The symbol represents the four elements. In your astrological chart it's the part of fortune where you will find most benefits in this life—a great indication of life purpose. Here, however, it reminds you of the work you have just done and that you're in a physical environment that gives form to all of the other Sephiroth above it. Color each quarter differently: yellow, red, blue, and green.

So now you have a Tree featuring planets and you have also added the relevant colors. All these images, together with the name, number, and general influences of the Sephira, are starting to build up a bigger picture.

Find Your Ruling Sephira

You are ruled by one of the Sephira—you can find it in the list below. Think about what your personality Sephira offers you as you consider its link with your astrological sign.

- Pisces is ruled by Kether.

- Aquarius is ruled by Chokmah.

- Capricorn is ruled by Binah.

- Sagittarius is ruled by Chesed.

- Aries and Scorpio are ruled by Geburah.

- The Sun is ruled by Tiphareth.

- Taurus and Libra are ruled by Netzach.

- Gemini and Virgo are ruled by Hod.

- Cancer is ruled by Yesod.

And Malkuth is ruled by your rising sign. If you know your rising sign, it will reveal your approach to living here on Earth.

Today's homework is to color the Tree. Sit with it and think about the link between the planets, colors, and Sephiroth, and what your ruling Sephira says about you.

Tomorrow is all about Yesod, so tonight take extra time to make a wish on the Moon before you go to sleep.

DAY 9

The Sephiroth: Yesod

*"I have a memory like an elephant.
In fact, elephants often consult me."*
Noel Coward

Pick an oracle or Tarot card, and in your journal write down what card it is and what it means.

I have used the above quote today not only because this is the Sephira of memory, but also because it illustrates beautifully how diverse and all-encompassing the Qabalah is.

Today's topic is Yesod, which has many associated symbols and among them is the elephant. Perhaps this initially seems bizarre, but of course it doesn't take much of a leap to realize this is because elephants never forget—and neither does Yesod.

- Yesod: The Foundation.

- Position on the Tree: Nine.

- Planet: The Moon.

- Archangel: Gabriel.

- Virtue: Independence.

- Vice: Idleness.

- Color: Violet.

- Incense: Jasmine.

- Body part: The genitals.

- Tarot cards: The four 9s.

Astral Planes: Beyond the Veil

In recent years there has been a great resurgence in all things ghostly, the paranormal, and mediumship. The "things that go bump in the night" are separated from our earthly world by a thin veil, in much the same way as Malkuth is separated from Yesod.

The next plane of existence, sometimes called the astral plane, is the domain of Yesod, and we cannot travel up from or down to Malkuth without moving past this plane and its worlds.

In their simplest forms, this is indeed where you find deceased relations waiting for you as their memories are still within you. However, Yesod has more important associations. This is where you meet your powerful subconscious mind, where you reach into the melting pot of all you've ever done to bring forward answers to help you in the here and now, as well as lessons that you might still have to work on.

I am all for living in the now, being positive, keeping those affirmations going to maintain direction and impetus toward your goals, but the reality is that you will have things you need to confront. Some people prefer to ignore them and try to move on, but all that does is push certain issues under the astral carpet until eventually you're not able to move without tripping over them.

This is the place where you give birth to all those thoughts, feelings, and emotions; the place you can visit to remind yourself of what's waiting for you but also what to be wary of and to work on before you go any further.

Yesod's association with the Moon reminds us that life itself moves in cycles. There is a time to move forward; a time to lie low; a time to talk; a time to remain silent; a time to remember; and a time to forget and move on. Yesod is called the foundation because it turns the wheels of the Universe to bring us what we want in the way we have seen it, felt it, and indeed worked for it.

Idleness is the vice linked to Yesod, as contentment can sometimes lead to us sitting back and changing nothing. Life is about keeping things moving and being open to change, and from that comes independence, as you are master of your own machine.

Gabriel is Yesod's angelic force. He is the Archangel of Water as this Sephira is associated with Cancer and emotional energy. He is also the Archangel whom we see at the Annunciation, when Mary is told that she is to be the mother of Christ. Here he sits in governance over the birth canal on the Tree of Life, ready to manifest your dreams.

The four 9s remind you that you are almost there—the hard work is done and you're just about to reap the benefits. But, as ever, there are warnings: don't give in to unnecessary worry and keep your images sharp, well defined, and clear. Look at the cards in your Tarot deck for extra information.

In your life Yesod is likely to show through cycles—those repeat performances that we all go through—and taking some time today to think about those is what's asked of you. What cycles or habits do you notice that work really well for you and which would you like to break free from?

What Yesod is not about is having regrets; it recognizes where you may have done things differently but all experiences are valid, workable with and, when you do work with them, the wheels turn again and the great mechanism of the universe brings forth new and exciting things.

Temples

Every Sephira has a temple within it—a place of beauty and, as with Malkuth, a place to go to begin magical journeys, for energy to be attracted into your life. The nature of remote Qabalah (studying without a teacher) means that entering these temples may not be the best thing to do, as each student has a unique way of experiencing them and the way they bring their energy to Earth. For that reason we will be visiting them later in Malkuth, viewing them from the safety of Earth. You will still feel their influence, but in a gentle way. Yesod has one of the most beautiful temples, made of silver and mother of pearl. You will see it in just a few days, along with the temples of Hod and Netzach.

Today's homework is to get yourself a Moon diary and look at the phases of the Moon. I'd like you to find out when she is waxing and when she is waning; when she is full and when she is new. Monitor how you feel when she's at each phase of the cycle, charting your emotions using the diary to see if she offers any insight into your behavior. During the three days before a new Moon, when she is called a dark Moon, please do not attempt any magic. This is simply because the Moon's energy is very low at this time.

Also reflect on your habits and cycles; think about the ideas you give birth to here on Earth, and which experiences you would rather not repeat.

DAY 10

The Sephiroth: Hod

*"I saw an angel in the marble and
carved until I set him free."*

MICHELANGELO

**Pick an oracle or Tarot card, and in your journal
write down what card it is and what it means.**

Today our subject is Hod. Let's start by taking a look at
its correspondences.

- Keyword: Splendor.

- Position on the Tree: Eight.

- Planet: Mercury.

- Archangel: Raphael.

- Virtue: Truthfulness.

- Vices: Falsehood; dishonesty.

- Color: Orange.

- Incense: Storax; white sandalwood.

- Body parts: The loins; the legs.

- Tarot cards: The four 8s.

Creating Images

"Imagine"—what a great word! It's an escape; it's a lottery win and lying about on golden beaches for some; for others it's meeting their soul mate, enjoying their perfect wedding, or having a baby; or perhaps it's seeing a product they've worked on now being available in a store. Everything that exists was once imagined.

We are often told to be careful what we wish for, and we should certainly take great care in the way we make our wishes. Details are important, and making sure you have thought things through is the world according to Hod. It also asks that you're honest about what you want and how you're going to get it.

This is the home of the intellect, of science and teaching, and sometimes teacher guides from the spiritual worlds will meet you here. Hod is also where you will find your Doorkeeper—a guide whose role is to protect your mind and keep you safe from false images and ideas that say more about the agenda of others than your own desires.

Hod governs ceremony and planning—how you go about the details of making things happen and who stands where and when. This is the organizational Sephira, but such is the nature of Hod and its associated planet, Mercury, that it's also very fluid and can sometimes go off on a tangent. Who hasn't had a great idea only to be sidelined by something sparkling in the distance? If you are feeling sidelined, meditating on Hod can put you back on track.

Raphael reminds you that your outer world is a reflection of your inner one. He is the Archangel of Air and as such knows that every thought becomes a thing. Calling upon him to help clear your mind is a useful thing to do. He is also seen in Hod as a guiding force that helps you release and heal thoughts you no longer need.

The four 8s in the Tarot pack will remind you that you can transcend your limitations, or your perceived limitations, with forethought, planning, and putting form around your ideas.

Balancing your thoughts and your feelings is one of the things that we as humans attempt to do. Netzach represents feelings and Hod symbolizes form, and if you look at your Tree of Life you will see that the path between them is the Tower card. If you veer toward over-thinking things or over-feeling, you can easily bring about the collapse of that Tower and you have to start to build it all over again.

An important lesson to be learned from Hod as you move up the Tree is that no Sephira acts alone. Each one is connected to its neighbors and, by association, to each and every one of the Sephiroth, just as you are fundamentally connected to all your fellow human beings.

Visualization: The Doorkeeper

Today is a day for visualization. This time you're going to look at that Doorkeeper of yours, find out who it is, and how they appear. You're doing this to protect your great ideas and to be less influenced by those whose ideas don't fall in line with yours. Your Doorkeeper often appears as someone very fierce—when you think about it, they would have to be. They are in a protective role, so often the way they look is simply enough for someone else's silly ideas to run off. Mine is an executioner, complete with leather mask–that explains a lot!

Before you begin, remember to set up for the visualization as you did previously, on Day 7. Then, after lighting your candle, as before begin breathing in a 4-2-4-2 pattern: breathe in, nice and deep, for four seconds. Hold it for two, breathe out for four seconds, then hold it for two again. Repeat a few times, each time relaxing more and more.

Are you ready? Now close your eyes. See yourself back in your forest (the same one you visited in the previous visualization, on Day 7), walking through the trees and into the clearing.

As you face the Tree you will see the door open. Walk in to Malkuth, look at the stained glass windows, the altar, the pillars, and the doors.

Smile as Sandalphon appears. Let him give you his blessing and ask him if you can meet your Doorkeeper. He laughs and reminds you that your Doorkeeper has always been with you. He asks you to turn around, slowly… and there is your Doorkeeper. They are like an old friend, happy to see you. Or should that be happy to be seen by you? Thank them for their presence. What do they look like? Why have they chosen to look that way?

They remind you that if you're feeling a little overwhelmed, you can ask them to cut away anything that isn't yours, to remove negativity that's built up through no fault of your own. You can also ask them to help bring clarity to a situation that needs certainty. Remember that they are more than they appear—your Doorkeeper often holds more knowledge than they're given credit for.

When it's time to leave, say your farewells. The Doorkeeper isn't going anywhere; you just won't be aware of them very often. If you wish, you can ask them to give you a sign in future to show that they are present—perhaps a sensation of touch.

Now thank Sandalphon and make your way out of Malkuth, into the clearing, and then into the forest once more.

When you are ready, bring your awareness back into the room. Slowly open your eyes, and wiggle your fingers and toes. If you wish, you can now make yourself refreshments.

Recording Your Journey

Now, as you did with the previous visualization, get out your journal and write down your experience. Here are some prompts to help you.

- If the Doorkeeper gave you their name—well done! Write it down.

- What were they wearing?

- What did they say to you?

- Could you make use of them more?

- What thoughts that clutter your mind don't belong to you?

- Do you need clarity in an emotional matter?

- Are your feelings overriding logic? Or is logic overriding your feelings?

The last thing I'm going to ask you to do today is to look at the four 8s in your Tarot deck. Ponder these images and what they mean to you.

Tomorrow we're moving on to Netzach, which is more of a "touchy-feely" Sephira than an intellectual one.

DAY 11

The Sephiroth: Netzach

"Mankind is governed more by feelings than by reason."

SAMUEL ADAMS

Pick an oracle or Tarot card, and in your journal write down what card it is and what it means.

Today we're going to get to know Netzach, the realm of feelings. Here are its correspondences.

- Keyword: Victory.

- Planet: Venus.

- Position on the Tree: Seven.

- Archangel: Haniel.

- Virtue: Unselfishness.

- Vice: Lust.

- Color: Green.

- Incense: Rose.

- Body parts: The pelvic area; the hips.

- Tarot cards: The four 7s.

Here we come to the domain of Venus. You would think she needs no introduction—surely it's all about love? In fact, the whole Tree is about love. Venus may have first dibs on the earthly expression of it, but the reality is that no Sephira holds anything other than love at its heart.

Netzach can often show itself in our most intimate relationships, as it's about our feelings and they are something that we humans wear on our sleeves. The balancing act between Hod and Netzach isn't always easy to maintain. If anything is going to be heavily weighted, it's usually the side that looks at feelings.

The keyword "Victory" that describes Netzach may seem an odd choice, but in this context it simply refers to victory over your feelings. This is not the same as being emotionally cold. It means that when you have feelings that seem overwhelming, you will know how to bring them under control. You can visit Hod and all its images, and remind yourself that logic has its place. With this in mind, you can think about what you're feeling and what can you do to deal with it all. And when you've done that, you can push it all out through Yesod to complete the process.

The Archangel associated with Netzach is Haniel. She wears beautiful dresses like a Greek goddess and has emeralds on her wingtips, as I see her anyway! She reminds you that peace, beauty, grace, and charm can go a very long way, but make no mistake, Haniel is also aware of the laws of nature and she also encourages you to bare your teeth should the need arise.

The four 7s show us the challenges in life that are brought about through a battle within—our feelings challenging us to get to the truth of how we *really* feel.

Art and music are represented in this Sephira. It's the inspiration for many people who are involved in these pursuits and home to spiritual guides who have an interest in helping you make the most of your own talents. Visiting Netzach can help clear the way if you're feeling blocked in an artistic project.

Netzach is where your personality meets your soul. Perhaps the heart of the matter is that what your personality thinks it should, could, or would have isn't in line with what your soul knows you can and will have, which creates inner conflict.

Nature is perfect in every way. Everything has its place in the ecosystem. Take roses, which bloom in all their beauty when they are ready—they look just as they should look and smell just as they should smell. Bugs sometimes eat into them, but bugs are part of nature, too, and they are only doing what bugs do. Then birds eat the bugs, which is what birds do. We are also creatures of nature. Being honest about your feelings is akin to acting like the rose, the bugs, and the birds. They don't stop to think or analyze, they simply do what they do. You may believe that's because they probably don't have the intellectual capacity to do so, and you have a point—but so does Netzach. You are already beautiful—as perfect as that rose—and you can achieve everything that you've incarnated to achieve, if only you listen to the truth of your feelings and unselfishly accept yourself as the whole being that you are.

Visualization: Lost and Hidden Truths

Today's visualization takes you to a past life to view where blocks have occurred or as yet undiscovered blessings lie. This exercise is very simple and can be done whenever you feel your question would be better answered by visiting a place that's deep in your "memory." You will be visiting Malkuth, where a mirror has been placed for you. This is the mirror of Yesod and in it you will see yourself in a former life.

Before you begin, remember to set up for the visualization as you did previously. Then, after lighting your candle, as before begin breathing in a 4-2-4-2 pattern: breathe in, nice and deep, for four seconds. Hold it for two, breathe out for four seconds, then hold it for two again. Repeat a few times, each time relaxing more and more.

Close your eyes and imagine that you are back in your forest. (It should be very easy to conjure up now, and will build quickly around you. Remember to immerse yourself in it completely.)

Move to your clearing when you're ready, then find the door and enter Malkuth. As you familiarize yourself with the temple again by looking at the pillars, the altar, and the windows, you notice a plinth has been placed in the center. Standing by it is Sandalphon, who asks you to come toward him.

Take your time and look around you. In front of the plinth is a mirror. This is the mirror of Yesod and it has been placed here for you and covered with a red velvet cloth.

Sandalphon asks you to stand on the plinth and face the mirror. When you're ready he tells you to pull the cloth away and see yourself in it as you were in a former life.

The mirror might just reflect back the image of the person you were or it might depict a scene from your life in that incarnation. Pay close attention to what you see.

Ask Sandalphon any questions that arise from what you see in the mirror. For example: Why do you feel a certain way around someone? Why do some situations just repeat themselves? And so on. Do not be afraid to ask anything that will help you to understand your feelings.

Once you have finished asking questions, thank Sandalphon for his presence and step off the plinth. Leave the temple and make your way into the clearing and into the forest.

When you are ready, bring your awareness back into the room. Slowly open your eyes, and wiggle your fingers and toes. If you wish, you can now make yourself refreshments.

Recording Your Journey

Now, as you did with the previous visualizations, take out your journal and write down your experience. Here are some prompts to help you.

- When you saw yourself in the mirror, were you male or female?

- What did you look like?

- What were you doing?

- Who else, if anyone, did you see?

- What period were you from?

- What answers did you get from your questions?

Tonight, I'd like you to think about what you were shown and why. Then look at the 7s in your Tarot deck, make some notes, and ponder this question: "What is my soul saying that my personality isn't quite hearing?"

Tomorrow we will be consolidating what we have learned so far.

DAY 12

Consolidating the Personality Triangle

"I finally got it all together, but I forgot where I put it."

ANON

Pick an oracle or Tarot card, and in your journal write down what card it is and what it means.

Tightening up what we've learned along the way is an important discipline to get into, so we're going to spend today consolidating what we have already learned. Take it from someone who has tried the other approach: consolidating helps you better understand where you are now, as well as how far you have come. We would normally do a consolidation after each path-working, but as that is beyond the scope of this book, we are going recap after each set of three Sephiroth.

If you look at your Tree, you will see that, leaving out Malkuth for the moment, it can be split into three triangles: at the top Binah, Chokmah, and Kether, which point upward; in the middle Tiphareth, Geburah, and Chesed, pointing downward; and at the bottom Yesod, Hod, and Netzach also pointing downward. Malkuth—"home sweet home"— is on its own at the very bottom, waiting to receive all the information from the other Sephiroth.

These triangles are known as the Supernals. The top one governs the big picture—humanity as a whole—and can be seen as the spiritual triangle. The middle triangle is about your intuition and your soul, as well as humanity, and is called the soul triangle. The bottom one is personality-led and it reflects not only your own personality, but also that of humanity. It is known as the personality triangle.

So, today we are going to consolidate your experiences with the personality triangle.

Getting Personal

The beauty of the Qabalah is that it brings its lessons into real life. It sits in front of you reminding you that it is *real*, not something you simply read about and ponder. Bearing that in mind, it's time to review what we've covered over the past few days.

(When you finish this 21-day course, I suggest you go back and revisit each Sephira, allowing at least a month to six weeks between them to fully get the benefit of each one's unique influence.)

Consolidation

Begin by asking yourself questions. Let your intuition flow; think about the planets, Sephiroth, Tarot cards, images, and visualizations you have recently encountered.

- Ask yourself again what your dream, your goal, is.

- Looking at each Sephira, how has it reflected in your life? Yesod—cycles; Hod—thoughts; Netzach—feelings.

- If you know your chart, look at the Moon, Mercury and Venus. What information do they give you?

- Arrange the following Tarot cards on a table in their relevant positions: the Tower horizontally; the Sun at a 45-degree angle on the left; the Star at a 45-degree angel on the right. Look at the cards, analyze them, and think about how they might work with the Sephira and in your life. Remember the example of the Tower card running between your thoughts and feelings—what does this tell you about your personality?

- Ask yourself whether or not there are cycles you could without. Are there those in your life who need to know how you truly feel, or perhaps you need to slow down to listen to them?

Now put it all together and come up with a statement that begins: From the personality Supernal I have learned…. Write this in your journal.

To help you finish this section, here's a visualization you can do when you've finished your consolidation.

Visualization: The Temples of Yesod, Hod, and Netzach

Before you begin, remember to set up for the visualization as you did previously. Then, after lighting your candle, as before begin breathing in a 4-2-4-2 pattern: breathe in, nice and deep, for four seconds. Hold it for two, breathe out for four seconds, then hold it for two again. Repeat a few times, each time relaxing more and more.

Are you ready? Now close your eyes. Make your way to your forest, the clearing and into Malkuth.

Sandalphon is waiting for you. He guides you to the pillars and you stand in front of them, ebony on your left, ivory on your right. As you face the pillars, you notice a curtain, with a thin veil hanging from the center.

Sandalphon asks you to watch, to look through the veil. At first you may see nothing, yet as you concentrate you begin to see a violet light, misty at first but then alive with color. Then an image of a Chinese pagoda appears. Its roof is made of silver and it has mother-of-pearl walls. This is the Temple of Yesod.

The garden has a lake with a half-moon bridge spanning it. The moon itself is reflected in the water. Is it full, new, waxing, or waning? Gabriel stands in the garden smiling at you, sending love.

The image fades and an orange light appears, again misty but soon clearing to reveal a frozen white wasteland, a blank canvas. As you watch, the Temple of Hod rumbles up through the ice. It is made of ice and is created from your thoughts, just as all things are created from our thoughts. Frozen into its walls are the 22 Major Arcana cards of the Tarot. Does any one card capture your attention more than any other?

Raphael stands looking at you. Make his image as clear as you can. Now this image fades and you will begin to see a bright emerald-green light. As its brightness wanes, a lush landscape appears with rolling green hills and an abundance of flowers in such colors as you've never seen before.

On a hill in the distance you see a Grecian temple. Outside there are two leopards guarding its entrance. This is the Temple of Netzach. Below the temple is a rose garden with many statues of Classical gods and goddesses.

Haniel is there. She smiles, and sends love and peace to you.

As this image in turn also fades, you slowly bring your attention back to the veil and to Malkuth. Sandalphon leads you back to the altar. You thank him for the time you have spent here and for allowing you to visit the temples of Yesod, Hod, and Netzach.

He asks you to leave and you go out into the clearing and then into the forest.

When you are ready, bring your awareness back into the room you're in. Slowly open your eyes, and wiggle your fingers and toes. As before, if you wish you can now make yourself refreshments.

Recording Your Journey

Now, as you did with the previous visualizations, take out your journal and write down your experience. I haven't included any prompts this time as by now I think you know how to do this. Just take your time recalling and describing this visualization, and enjoy your very special, magical journey.

Tomorrow it's on to the next triangle as we start with Tiphareth.

DAY 13

The Sephiroth: Tiphareth

*"The pursuit of truth and beauty is a
sphere of activity in which we are permitted
to remain children all our lives."*

ALBERT EINSTEIN

**Pick an oracle or Tarot card, and in your journal
write down what card it is and what it means.**

Today we are exploring Tiphareth, a place of healing energy.
Here are its correspondences.

- Keyword: Beauty.

- Planet: The Sun.

- Position on the Tree: Six.

- Archangel: Michael.

- Virtue: Devotion to the Great Work.

- Vice: Pride.

- Color: Yellow.

- Incense: Frankincense.

- Body part: The breasts.

- Tarot cards: The four 6s.

This Sephira sits in the center of the Tree and is the balancing point. It's where we first encounter the energy of the soul on the climb up from Malkuth. (Of course, that also means it's where the soul gives way for the personality on the way down!)

Tiphareth is a place of great healing and love, as well as of sacrifice—for what greater love can you show for another than giving something up so that they can blossom? But sacrifice is not a prerequisite. It's simply that we usually experience soul energy in the act of helping others, whether or not that involves making a sacrifice. Who or what would you sacrifice everything for?

The Christ force is often attributed to this Sephira—that's the force, not the man. It's a healing energy and a sacrificial one, too, of course, but for me it's a place I love to go to when I am worn out and feeling in need of a top-up of energy. I meditate and drift off to sleep suffused in its energy, accepting the healing and restorative aspects of this lovely Sephira.

The word "beauty" reminds you that there is beauty in everything if you look for it. Sometimes you have to look very hard, but it's always there. If you try to see beauty, then beauty will be reflected back to you. You may have heard the term "soul decision"—this is where those are made, and seeing the beauty in everything will help you make them.

Tiphareth is also a place where your soul learns from those who have gone before it. You may experience the feeling that someone is watching over you or that a specific piece of knowledge is being put your way. Teachers, both earthly and spiritual, often appear when you are working with this Sephira.

Knowledge is a wonderful thing and as you climb the Tree you will see just how much there is to learn, and how far you have come. This inevitably leads to a feeling of achievement, but this must not be allowed to swell into pride, the vice of Tiphareth, as it warns against the puffed-up pride of superiority. Humility and your devotion to the work ahead will see you through.

The Archangel is Michael, but sometimes people see Raphael here, too. Raphael is renowned for his healing qualities, so that makes sense. For me, though, fiery Michael suits the element of this Sephira and its reflection of Kether, the Likeness of God. Michael is also a healer but he deals with more deep-rooted injuries than Raphael.

The Tarot cards remind us that through hard work and devotion, rewards will come. They suggest that Tiphareth's strength lies in taking up a challenge, working with it, and being victorious.

As the Sun governs Tiphareth it's easy to link this planet—strictly speaking a luminary—with the experience of the Sephira. The Sun shines on you as you reach for your higher good, the part of you that wants to respond and act from as high a level as you can. When you act from your soul level you feel great!

This balancing point is a wonderful space to be in. When was the last time you felt so balanced? What do you do to maintain balance in your life? Like most people, the answer may be an occasional night out with friends. Is that enough?

I think it helps, but maybe you need something that will give you a little more spiritual energy.

Visualization: Chakra-balancing

This visualization is all about pushing energy around some of the chakras–wheels of spinning energy that are situated in the energy body. (There are seven main chakras, located from the crown of the head down through the body to the perineum.) By helping the energy to move, you can bring the body back into balance. Think of it as being akin to riding a bike: the only way to keep it moving forward is to maintain your balance.

Before you begin, set up for the visualization as you did previously. Then, after lighting your candle, as before begin breathing in a 4-2-4-2 pattern: breathe in, nice and deep, for four seconds. Hold it for two, breathe out for four seconds, then hold it for two again. Repeat a few times, each time relaxing more and more.

This time there's no forest. (I know you'll miss it, but you'll be back there soon!)

So let's begin. Close your eyes and see a white light around you. Make it as pure as you can. Imagine a sphere of light above your head. Make it about the size of an apple and brilliant white. Turn up the light even more so that it's blue-white, sparkling and alive with energy. This is your higher self.

Now imagine there's a lotus flower on the crown of your head. This is the crown chakra. Watch as the lotus petals slowly unfurl. Make them open wider.

Next visualize a rosebud between your eyebrows, in the center of your forehead. This is where the "third-eye" chakra is located. Watch the rose gradually open out into a full bloom.

Now see a rosebud on your throat, where the throat chakra resides, and let it slowly open up.

Next move down to your heart area, the home of the heart chakra. Again see a rosebud resting there and gradually unfurling.

When you've done that, let the light move down through your legs and out through the soles of your feet. Extend the light across your shoulders and out through the palms of your hands. So now you're a being of light, as it flows in to the crown of your head, down through your body, and out through your feet and the palms of your hands.

Feel the light rebalance you, pushing away any gray bits—see them go—and replacing all your stagnant energy with balanced and vibrant energy.

When you're ready, return the light to your heart chakra. Imagine it glowing golden and see the beauty that is you; feel the beauty that is you; feel the balance that is you. Let the golden light vibrate. Now push it up through your throat chakra into your third eye, then through the crown chakra, and back into the sphere above your head.

Push the sphere into the sky and let it reconnect you to the Universe. Next visualize all those rosebuds and the lotus flower closing their petals, and the chakras returning to their natural state. These energy points will now feel recharged and working clearer, helping you to feel the same.

You know the drill! When you are ready, bring your awareness back into the room you're in. Slowly open your eyes, and wiggle your fingers and toes. As before, if you wish you can now make yourself refreshments.

Recording Your Journey

Now, as you did with the previous visualizations, take out your journal and write down your experience. Make notes, thinking about how you felt. What other things did you see? What thoughts came to mind? What challenges now seem less of drama?

You can do this exercise whenever you feel in need of an energy boost.

Tomorrow we're moving on to Geburah, so get some rest!

DAY 14

The Sephiroth: Geburah

"To go from mortal to Buddha, you have to put an end to karma, nurture your awareness, and accept what life brings."

BODHIDHARMA

Pick an oracle or Tarot card, and in your journal write down what card it is and what it means.

Today we are exploring Geburah, which is often associated with karma. Here are its correspondences.

- Keywords: Severity; strength.

- Planet: Mars.

- Position on the Tree: Five.

- Archangel: Khamael.

- Virtues: Energy; courage.

- Vice: Cruelty; destruction.

- Color: Red.

- Incense: Tobacco.

- Body part: The right arm.

- Tarot cards: The four 5s.

The ruby-red sphere of Geburah makes many people wonder just what karma has in store for them, but Geburah isn't punitive, it's a cleansing process. Here you recognize just what has to happen to help you move on. Remember, you're in the land of the soul's journey, so maybe some of the decision won't sit comfortably with your personality, but your soul knows what's right.

Karma is neither negative nor positive, it simply *is*. It's an equal or opposite reaction to decisions *you*—and only you— have made. Accepting that responsibility will help you work with this highly effective Sephira. Geburah is also home to the Lords of Karma—beings who have an interest in what you create and negate.

On the Tree of Life, Geburah is one up from Hod. Where Hod is your individual thoughts, Geburah is the power to make them happen, as your soul puts on its cheerleader's hat and urges you on. Geburah can destroy what no longer serves you well, all in the name of elevating you and bringing your will into being.

Red is the color of Geburah for good reason—it's passionate and fires up enthusiasm. Red is also the color of fire, which is a purifying force. Just ask any passing phoenix as it rises renewed and splendid from the flames that bring it rebirth!

Mars is Geburah's ruling planet and again we see the theme of fire. A warring planet and the ruler of Aries, this god governs with martial law: he's the colonel-in-chief, ready to do battle on your behalf to achieve your goals.

In the Temple of Geburah, negative karma can be cut away or lasered off where appropriate, but don't be fooled—whilst you see it removed in the temple, the hard work will, as always, be done in Malkuth.

Khamael is the Archangel of Geburah. Strong and courageous, he is also the Archangel of Justice. He tests your convictions, asks you to show your true intentions, and purifies your thoughts through your acceptance of the consequences of your actions. He also tempers the energy of the lightning flash as it descends the Tree of Life (see Day 2), adding more when it's needed, holding back when it's not. He is karma in motion. Take care to do that yourself. If you assume that this power is yours to wield in any way you see fit, you might just discover that things don't go according to plan. Overuse of Geburah can sometimes lead to destructive forces being unleashed. Remember the consequences of your actions.

The number five in the Tarot can often be seen as trouble, a bothersome influence that demands you take action. It can, of course, mean you are releasing that energy and coming to terms with the root of the problem, but when the Tarot 5s appear, think Geburah—think about what you can do to move things along. What do you need to face and what might need cutting away?

For me this Sephira has always been one I approach with extra respect and reverence, just as I would a fire or a molten-lava flow. However, recognizing when you're in Geburah isn't always easy, as anger clouds your vision red. But the simplest answer is obvious—you're in it when you can't see for anger and frustration.

Visualization: Cutting the Cord

To help you ponder where you might remove something that needs to go or that is unnecessarily holding back your progress, I suggest that you do the following exercise of cutting the cord, which will encourage the process of letting go.

Before you begin, set up for the visualization as you did previously. Then, after lighting your candle, as before begin breathing in a 4-2-4-2 pattern: breathe in, nice and deep, for four seconds. Hold it for two, breathe out for four seconds, then hold it for two again. Repeat a few times, each time relaxing more and more.

Close your eyes and slowly conjure up an image of the person or situation you're attached to. You can envisage this as a cord that exists between you, or even as a sparkly silver rope.

The thickness of the cord or rope reflects the thickness of your bond with the person or situation. How thick is your bond? Obviously if it's very thick cord or rope, it may take longer to cut than a wispy string.

Take a good look at the cord. How sparkly is it? Or maybe it's not sparkly at all? Does it form a chain? Is it made of silk? What does the appearance of the cord tell you about this situation?

Recognize that this attachment wasn't forced upon you—you played your part in forming it. Spend a moment thanking the energy this cord has brought you. No doubt you have learned lessons and future routes will be clearer.

Now cut the cord or rope. You can use whatever method you wish: it may be scissors or a knife, or you could tear it, snap it, or even get industrial cutters on it if you need them!

You must now fill the space you've left, by cutting your ties with your chosen person or situation, with love. Then seal the area with white or pink light, and by so doing seal your energetic body.

When you are ready, come back to your usual state of awareness. Slowly open your eyes, and wiggle your fingers and toes. As before, if you wish you can now make yourself refreshments.

Recording Your Journey

Now take out your journal and record your images and how you felt. It's not uncommon for someone on the other end of your cord to feel something as well as you, so don't be surprised if they get in touch to try to reconnect with you.

It's not easy to say no to people or to cut them out of your life, but it's even tougher to continue on a path you know is no good for you. Be strong, ask for Khamael's help, and remember that Geburah works best when you have courage.

Tomorrow we will move on to the benevolent realm of Chesed.

DAY 15

The Sephiroth: Chesed

"Think carefully before asking for
justice. Mercy might be safer."
MASON COOLEY

Pick an oracle or Tarot card, and in your journal write down what card it is and what it means.

Today's topic is Chesed, the Sephira of Divine love. Here are its correspondences.

- Keyword: Mercy.

- Planet: Jupiter.

- Position on the Tree: Four.

- Archangel: Tzadkiel.

- Virtue: Obedience.

- Vices: Bigotry; gluttony.

- Color: Blue.

- Incense: Cedar.

- Body part: The left arm.

- Tarot cards: The four 4s.

The sapphire-blue Sephira balances the ruby red of Geburah. Its mercy and divine love encourage growth and put opportunities your way. This isn't about fancying that guy from Accounts; it's Divine love—the love your soul has for humanity even though sometimes you're not sure just why it's doing things the way that it does.

Jupiter governs this Sephira from a place of benevolence in his guise as a heavenly father figure. The planet of old-fashioned good luck, Jupiter is also the planet of your higher ideals. Chesed is about your soul's values, and you can see how it's perfectly placed to align you with your higher self.

Here we find the Lords of Peace, who encourage us to find peaceful solutions before the need to use any other forces.

But sometimes the temptation is to be so peace-loving that you may not see what's truly going on, so the great Lords of Karma will alert you and wake you up.

Chesed is the first of the soul Sephiroth. Its energy comes direct from Binah and as such it's Chesed's job to start to put real form around your goal—that's why it's so exciting and can get carried away with itself. It's a royal Sephira, which may be why so many royal families wear deep, rich blue in their ceremonial robes.

If you were royalty, you would surely want to rule with a guiding hand that was merciful and benevolent, or perhaps like a parent keeping the family on the straight and narrow. This Sephira reminds us that we have a role to play in the lives of others as well as in our own—it encourages us to be all that we can be. Obedience here means obedience to your soul and spiritual values.

Tzadkiel is the Archangel of Chesed. He is associated with magic and the masters who populate this Sephira. Often seen as the Angel of Good Luck, Tzadkiel believes that good luck is earned.

The Masters appear in Chesed—higher beings who have chosen to help humanity—but remember that they are from our ranks, and will know what you're going through and encourage you to keep going, trekking up the mountain to reach your goals. Philosophy, art, and education are of interest to them and they often take on large groups of people to help them on their path.

Love is the vision of Chesed. It's a Sephira of humility and for me it's simply the most beautiful of all: generous, loving, kind, and somewhere to go when you miss your father and want that sort of guidance.

The Tarot 4 are cards that offer rewards—they are good-news cards and when you see them they offer gifts for a job well done. Make no mistake, however. If you visit Chesed to ask for things, you *will* get them, but Chesed will demand payment in some way. For me it's about receiving confirmation that I'm on the right track, not assuming that I've been good and demanding a present. That won't work!

Chesed Awareness

What brings you peace? Where do you find that moment when you feel at one, not only with yourself, but with everything around you? When you climb the Tree and begin to reach these higher branches the fruit is sweeter, but you mustn't forget what makes it all grow or the reason it's there in the first place.

Earthing your Tree of Life is important, so today is about remembering when you were with the Elementals a few days ago, and finding a way to incorporate all of the Tree you've discovered so far into your experience of Chesed.

Acts of Random Kindness (A.R.K.)

Acting from pure love, from mercy, from your higher self, and doing so consciously, constitutes today's homework. Such acts needn't be anything huge. For example, you could fix dinner for your partner or your parents—something they aren't expecting—as a little expression of your love and appreciation for all that they do for you.

However, the best way to do this is to perform a truly random act of kindness for a stranger, and to do it anonymously. I have a friend in Australia who runs a great teaching night a few times a month. At each session she holds a raffle, and the prizes are things she can gather together or sometimes gifts that kind souls bring her. During the evening, she collects the raffle-ticket money and asks those who come along to suggest people they know who are struggling financially and having a hard time. Then after the raffle, she the pulls names out of a hat to decide where the money raised goes. This is then put in an envelope and given to the person in need, sometimes anonymously and sometime with "Anam Cara" (soul friend) written on it, but never with her own name on it. This is a fine example of a gift from many hearts making a difference in one person's life—a true Chesed experience.

So, what difference could *you* make today? It doesn't have to be a big deal, but look out for your opportunity and when you see it, take it.

Tomorrow we are going to consolidate what we have learned so far about Tiphareth, Geburah, and Chesed.

DAY 16

Consolidating the Soul Triangle

"Begin to see yourself as a soul with a body rather than a body with a soul."

WAYNE DYER

Pick an oracle or Tarot card, and in your journal write down what card it is and what it means.

It's time for more consolidation today as we look again at Tiphareth, Geburah, and Chesed.

The soul is of course not perfect in and of itself, as it's still fed by the spiritual triangle, but it's a long way up the Tree and is making decisions from higher energy as well as connecting to some highly evolved beings in order to help you.

Remember that everything will manifest eventually in Malkuth, so the purer your intention up the Tree, the purer the result at the bottom of it—your goals come through pretty much as you planned with no sticky situations to negotiate.

The past few days— in fact, since you started this journey— have been full-on and so I'd now like to offer you a little breathing space before we move on to the final set of Sephira. Remember that this is an introduction to the Qabalah and you can take your time when you work through these pages—take all the time you need.

Your soul may have given you information that you're not so keen on. It could be challenging, and perhaps hard work looms, but if you're coming at it from a point of truth and honesty with yourself, any changes will be met with opportunities and balance will of course be restored.

Consolidation

Begin by asking yourself questions. Let your intuition flow, and think about the planets, Sephiroth, Tarot cards, images, and visualizations you have recently encountered.

• Ask yourself again what your dream, your goal is.

- Looking at each Sephira, how has it reflected in your life? Tiphareth—balance; Geburah—what needs cutting away; Chesed—opportunities.

- If you know your chart, look at the Sun, Mars and Jupiter. What information do they give you?

- Put the following cards on a table in their relevant positions: Lust/Strength horizontally; Adjustment/Justice at a 45-degree angle on the left; the Hermit at a 45-degree angel on the right. Look at the cards, analyze them and think about how they might work with the Sephira and in your life. Lust runs between Geburah and Chesed—it asks you to take the beast, to take control, and to ride your dream all the way to manifestation. What does this tell you about your soul?

- What goes, what stays, what balancing act are you performing?

Remember that even as you work on the soul level it all must be earthed. How is the energy coming back to Earth?

Ask questions, let your intuition flow, think "planet, Sephira, card, images, meditations, and experience," and put it all together to come up with a statement that begins: From the soul Supernal I have learned....

Ask yourself again what your dream, your goal is.

Visualization:
The Mountain of Wisdom

To help you finish this section, here's a visualization you can do when you've finished your consolidation.

Before you begin, set up for the visualization as you did previously. Then after lighting your candle, as before begin breathing in a 4-2-4-2 pattern: breathe in, nice and deep, for four seconds. Hold it for two, breathe out for four seconds, then hold it for two again. Repeat a few times, each time relaxing more and more.

Close your eyes and make your way to your forest, the clearing, and into the Tree to Malkuth. Sandalphon is waiting for you. He guides you to the pillars, and you stand in front of them: ebony on your left, ivory on your right. As you face the pillars you see a curtain, with a thin veil hanging from the center.

Sandalphon asks you to watch, to look through the veil. The violet light of Yesod gives way to the green of Netzach and then the golden yellow light of Tiphareth fades in. As the light clears you see rolling green hills and on one of the hills, a cross; in the distance there is a white marbled cathedral of simple lines, bathed in a rainbow.

The archangel Michael stands before it, splendid in his coat of many colors and reminding you that it takes a spectrum of different energies to form the whole being. The image fades and you begin to see a ruby-red light. As it melts away a castle keep appears, made from iron with red walls that seem to be hewn from rubies. You glimpse through a window and within you see a room with a black-and-white floor, a chair in the center, and 42 others surrounding it in a horseshoe shape.

Khamael stands there, looking fierce, ready for battle. He reminds you that sometimes you must stand your ground. As his image slowly fades, the sapphire-blue of Chesed appears and you hear a wind whistling around you. The blue light fades in turn to reveal a mountain top with a sapphire-blue building at its peak. Climbing the mountain is a line of pilgrims making their way up to the temple in devotion, with another line going down, smiling at the success of their pilgrimage. In the garden you may see some masters—do you recognize any of them? Tzadkiel is also there, resplendent in his robes. He appears as an old man—wise and ready to share his wisdom. When you're ready, let this image fade and bring yourself back to Malkuth.

Sandalphon guides you back to the altar. Thank him and make your way out of the temple and into the clearing, then back into the forest.

Now when you are ready, bring your awareness back into the room you're in. Slowly open your eyes, and wiggle your fingers and toes. As before, if you wish you can now make yourself refreshments.

Recording Your Journey

Now, as you did with the previous visualizations, take out your journal and write down your experience. Make notes about what you saw, felt, thought, and want to get started on right away!

Eat well, rest, drink lots of water, and keep lighting your candles and burning incense in your home—all things that will help maintain your energy. Be good to yourself.

Tomorrow we're going to start looking at the final triangle, which is the one primarily concerned with your spiritual self. The very nature of the concepts can sometimes be obtuse, but trust that the energy will go where it's needed and the knowledge will be there when it's necessary to use it.

DAY 17

The Sephiroth: Binah

"Don't believe what your eyes are telling you.
All they show is limitation. Look with your
understanding, find out what you already
know, and you'll see the way to fly."
RICHARD BACH

Pick an oracle or Tarot card, and in your journal write down what card it is and what it means.

Our topic today is Binah, which represents the eternal feminine principle. Here are its correspondences:

- Keyword: Understanding.

- Planet: Saturn.

- Position on the Tree: Three.

- Archangel: Tzaphkiel.

- Virtue: Silence.

- Vice: Avarice.

- Color: Black.

- Incense: Myrrh.

- Body part: The right side of the face.

- Tarot cards: The four 3s.

The Great Mother

Binah is called the Great Mother. She is the cosmic Goddess, where life begins and ends; she is the great sea from where we all spring.

The keyword is "understanding" because without understanding, everything you learn, all the knowledge you attain, is worth nothing, and Binah brings about that understanding, especially of universal truths, as she sits so high up the Tree. She highlights questions that we all have, such as: What is our purpose? Why are we here? How can we serve? She offers the opportunity to understand ourselves and our place in the cosmos.

Binah turns both knowledge (Chokmah) and wisdom (Chesed) into understanding. Knowledge is something we constantly seek; wisdom is sharing what we have learned. But the alchemy of putting them together, as Binah does, truly produces a deep understanding of what we are about.

From the top of the Tree comes the seed of an idea. It's then given the energy of Chokmah, but it's here in Binah that it's given life, as Binah is the womb, the cosmic soup where shape is given and sent out to be all that it can be.

Saturn is the planet that governs Binah, his rings keeping things in order. Astrologically he is the planet of control and of time, and his cycle deals with the beginnings and endings that we all share. At around the age of about 28 to 30, we all experience our Saturn return, which is a time when we wonder what our life is all about and often make career changes. But more often, Binah shakes us up, itching to bring us a greater understanding of who we are and what our purpose is, and we see a new way of being ahead of us. It's a time when we realize that this is it, everything is down to us, and we take charge.

Binah is a tough taskmaster. This Sephira understands when her children need to fly the nest and will push them out, knowing they will be fine. But they must find their own way, safe in the knowledge that Binah will be there should they need support and, of course, she is ready to remind them of the rules. But she will also stand by the sea, weeping as she watches her children leave. Binah also symbolizes sorrow.

Tzaphkiel is the Archangel of Binah. He protects you from strife, and should be called upon whenever you feel things are little too full-on—perhaps when you are in need of some support dealing with what seems like a massive change that you think you might not be able to handle. He brings clarity to what's really going on, what the changes are about. He also shows you how you can learn from them and work with them, rather than let them take over.

The four 3s of the Tarot are strong structures—a triangle is stronger than a square—but hard work is required to put structure around your goal.

One of the things I particularly like about Binah is its silence. In saying nothing you can say so much. Binah is a quiet place, which may be why understanding comes. Stopping amidst a storm will show you just where the storm originated and what must happen for calmer seas to come.

Silence is Golden

Today's exercise is deceptively effective—it may seem like something and nothing—but I do know of many students who find this a tough thing to do.

It's very simply *being silent.*

If you could do it for half a day that would be great—in fact it would be amazing! Some can't do it for ten minutes! The purpose of the silence is to allow your inner chatter to wear itself out, to stop going on about phone contracts and cat litter, to finally let the noise of your inner personality die down and begin to listen with more clarity to your soul and your spirit.

You don't have to sit crossed-legged in meditation—in fact it's best if you don't. You should just *be.* Wander by the ocean if you can, as the sound of the waves and the motion of the ocean will help you empty your mind. No plugging-in your headphones and listening to some tunes! Remember: the exercise is about silence, not about not talking. Silence is what is required.

When you find the place where noise dies down and reach the heaven of no internal chatter and no external distractions,

I promise that you will feel more connected to the Universe than during any meditation. And from it will come a greater understanding of yourself—what happens next and what choices need to be made. You are Binah, you are the Great Mother, you can let go and become Goddess.

When you feel you've done enough, write down your experience. Was it tougher than you thought? What information came from your soul? Do you now recognize just how much your mind witters on all the time?

Next time you're in a conversation and you're not sure what someone is really trying to say to you, rather than pitching in, leave them to talk things out. Let them reach the point where they finally start listening to their soul and watch as they come up with their own answers. Then both you and they can finally understand what it was they needed all along. Silence is a very, very powerful tool.

Tomorrow you're off to meet Binah's other half, Chokmah. Relish today's silence as Chokmah holds the remote control and is about to change the channel!

DAY 18

The Sephiroth: Chokmah

"He dares to be a fool, and that is the first step in the direction of wisdom."

JAMES HUNEKER

Pick an oracle or Tarot card, and in your journal write down what card it is and what it means.

Today our subject is Chokmah, the eternal masculine principle. Here are its correspondences.

- Keyword: Wisdom.

- Planet: Uranus.

- Position on the Tree: Two.

- Archangel: Ratziel.

- Virtue: Devotion.

- Vices: Force; disorganization.

- Color: Gray.

- Incense: Musk.

- Body part: The left side of the face.

- Tarot cards: The four 2s.

The Great Father

Sitting opposite Binah on the Tree of Life is Chokmah: the God-force as man, the life force, the divine spark that initiates an idea, that feeds life in all is forms. Of course, it would be nothing without its counterpart, the receptivity of Binah. In this way the Tree reminds you once more that no Sephira works totally independently of any other.

Wisdom is its keyword—wisdom that just *is*. It's there as an accumulation of all that has gone before and, as the higher aspect of Chesed, this fatherly wisdom is one the spirit has gained from the soul's journey, but it also holds all it has learned from Kether.

Chokmah has a lot of energy to give; it's enthusiastic, promotes a lust for life, and applies logic to see where it should be moving. It's science and discovery; it's pure force in action waiting for Binah to give it form.

Zapping things into action, into being, Chokmah asks us to make that choice—what plans need an extra push? It's creative ideas applied with logic that could give birth to a new way of doing things or take your plans in a more beneficial direction. Chokmah throws the switch to "on."

I know that by now you are probably feeling confused. The nature of this upper Sephira is very abstract—it is more conceptual than Sephiroth at other levels. But one thing I do know is that if you trust that Chokmah can bring moments of pure inspiration—genius even— you will receive and hear him when he does.

If the Sephira above, Kether, is calm and motionless, Chokmah is where the first ripple of movement appears and the whole of the Universe begins to manifest. He is therefore also disruptive if not given form from Binah. Imagine you have an idea—it's pure genius—but you do nothing with it.

So it bothers you at night, nags you, you get no sleep, and then you finally get around to doing something with it, but someone else has beaten you to it. Don't let this happen! Hear Chokmah, use Chokmah.

Uranus is the planet assigned to Chokmah and finding him in your natal chart will bring you personal information. This planet can be disruptive but, like its Qabalistic counterpart, it can bring logical solutions that seem to come out of the blue. Wherever you find Uranus in your chart you're likely to find a part of your life that always seems to be in state of flux, but also a part in which you're at your most creative. The zodiac wheel itself is a symbol for Chokmah, an ever-changing theatre of inspiration, planetary movement, and possibilities waiting to be uncovered.

Ratziel is the archangel associated with Chokmah. He guides the creative force and is the keeper of mysteries. Some also place Jophiel here. Both archangels have links to Adam and Eve and their expulsion from the Garden of Eden; that must have been a shock for them but they had to get creative in order to survive!

The four 2s are Chokmah's Tarot cards, representing balance brought about by two energies working together rather than one trying to do it all on its own. The 2s remind you that in order to feel whole, both yin and yang should be present, polarity in its purest form.

We're already connected; sometimes all it takes is something or someone to switch us on.

Vision Board

You're now going to create a vision board by working through the creative inspiration you already have waiting for you, using your inner wisdom and letting it flow down through the Tree to help you manifest your dreams. In the role of guiding father, the energy of Chokmah can, and will, begin a process that energizes your desires and sends them on their way with sparkles and glitter!

Begin by getting a piece of US-ledger- (A3-) or US-letter- (A4-) size board (use a colored one if you like—get creative). Now look at that blank sheet. There's nothing on it, it's devoid of any influences at all. You're the one who decides what goes on it.

You may have used a vision board before and you may be anxious to get to cutting out pictures of the things you wish to manifest, such as ponies and sports cars— but not so fast! This time things are different. If you desire ponies and sports cars that's just fine, but the starting point here is energy. I want you to stare at the board. Then close your eyes, see the board in your mind's eye, and stare at it from that viewpoint.

Now let your subconscious mind put the ideas on it. Let your inner Chokmah show you the way, let it light up the paper and see what you see. Give yourself some time—the result may even surprise you.

Next, open your eyes and simply write on the board what you saw or, if you're the artistic sort, draw it—in fact even if you don't consider yourself artistic, draw it anyway.

Now you can get to the picture part of the process. Cut out images that fit your vision. When you've done that, fill the sheet with energetic additions such as glitter and maybe the occasional tiny crystal or two—anything that represents your desire to have your vision plugged in. Take your time, make yourself plenty of tea or coffee, bring out your cookie tin, and make a day of it.

Tonight is about dreams. Watch those dreams, for to dream is what makes you such a special being and it's where you connect to your Source and it to you.

Tomorrow we reach the top of the Tree of Life. What an amazing journey it's been, elevating yourself from the dense world of Malkuth all the way up to the meringue-whipped airiness of the highest triangle, and Kether!

DAY 19

The Sephiroth: Kether

"Give me a robe, put on my crown; I have Immortal longings in me."
WILLIAM SHAKESPEARE

Pick an oracle or Tarot card, and in your journal write down what card it is and what it means.

Our topic today is Kether, the pinnacle of the Tree of Life. Here are its correspondences.

- Keyword: Crown.

- Planet: Neptune.

- Position on the Tree: One.

- Archangel: Metatron.

- Virtue: Completion of the Great Work.

- Color: Brilliant white.

- Incense: Ambergris.

- Body part: The cranium.

- Tarot cards: The four aces.

From your new stopping place you might think that Malkuth is the highest Sephira of all. Maybe it is? Perhaps you have reached the root of Tree rather than it's highest branch, and where you live now in Malkuth is the fruit? Kether is a reflection of Malkuth and vice versa; they represent the root and the top of many trees to come, more shapes adding to the magic that is the ever-expanding Tree of Life.

For now, though, let's consider Kether in the position of the highest of the Sephira, a pure place where there is nothing: no form, no force, nothing tangible at all—and yet it feeds the entire Tree.

It's a tough place to see any symbols and by its very nature Kether shifts and loses you in its mists. This is the personality Sephira of all our Piscean friends, and if you have any of those you will know that sometimes they themselves aren't quite sure which way is up! But, like them, Kether has an innate sense of spirit, a connection that isn't tangible or definable, it just *is*.

There's much debate about planetary rulership for Kether. Some will say Uranus is its ruler, others Pluto. But for me Neptune is the only planet that brings the qualities of Kether alive. Neptune's nature is to lose himself in order to find what he is looking for and to suddenly come out with the answer. This is also the planet of the mystic, the seeker of magical knowledge.

Kether's keyword is crown, a reference among other things to where it sits on your body, just above your head. Think about that for a moment. Trying to understand the concepts of Kether may sometimes feel like trying to grab a cloud: you know it's there but you can't quite get your hands on it. So maybe you're not supposed to. Perhaps all you should do is know it's there?

The archangel associated with Kether is Metatron. For me he always appears as a small child but to others he is enormous.

He is said to be the closest to the Source, God, whatever you choose to call the Divine. Metatron is his right-hand man, the Prince of Archangels. His help is often needed when you are struggling with concepts and ideas that are just beyond the veil. When you know something is solvable but you just can't get through that candy floss, marshmallow moment... enter Metatron.

The four Tarot aces really don't need much of an introduction; they are the first rush of energy of the suits Fire, Earth, Air, and Water, reminding you that in Kether the elements of Malkuth are far from forgotten.

Visualization: The Tree of Life and the Body

As this is a special day it seems only fitting to do a visualization that will remind you just how far you've come and will go some way to reinforcing the Tree of Life in your mind and reminding you of where it sits symbolically on the body.

Before you begin, set up for the visualization as you did previously. Then after lighting your candle, as before begin breathing in a 4-2-4-2 pattern: breathe in, nice and deep, for four seconds. Hold it for two, breathe out for four seconds, then hold it for two again. Repeat a few times, each time relaxing more and more.

Close your eyes and imagine a glowing Tree of Life in front of you. Look at the Sephiroth, see them glowing colorfully and vibrating with energy.

Now turn your back on the Tree, and put your spine against the middle pillar. First make sure your feet are firmly rooted in Malkuth—see them anchored in the earth, your home for now.

Now focus your attention on your groin area. Visualize Yesod glowing violet and silver. Moving up and across your body, next see the orange light of Hod sitting on your right hip. When you're ready, move to the emerald Sephira of Netzach on your left hip. Now progress to the yellow sphere of Tiphareth, over your solar plexus and heart. Next envision the ruby-red of Geburah on your right arm followed by the sapphire blue of Chesed on your left. Then to the right of your head, see and feel the black Sephira of Binah, and to your left, the gray circle of Chokmah. Finally, imagine brilliant-white Kether above your head. Sit with this image.

Do any of the Sephiroth appear dull, maybe in need of some extra energy? If any do, send them that extra energy, down through the Tree, using the lightning-flash path to balance them all. Remember, no Sephira works on its own.

Starting with Kether, move to Chokmah, onto Binah and toward Chesed; next across to Geburah and over to Tiphareth, through to Netzach; now back to Hod, toward Yesod and back into Malkuth; and through your feet into the earth, where you can secure and ground your energy.

When you are ready, bring your awareness back into the room. Slowly open your eyes, and wiggle your fingers and toes. As before, if you wish you can now make yourself refreshments.

Recording Your Journey

Now, as you did with the previous visualizations, take out your journal and write down your experience. Make notes, think about how you felt. What thoughts came to mind?

Well done! It's time to celebrate as you have come a very long way. And after tomorrow's consolidation, I will show you how to continue on the journey at your own pace.

DAY 20

Consolidating the Spiritual Triangle

*"People turn to Spirit when their
foundations are shaking, only to discover
that it is Spirit that is shaking them."*

ANON

**Pick an oracle or Tarot card, and in your journal
write down what card it is and what it means.**

So, here we are at the last triangle and, of course, it's the
spiritual one, and our subject for today.

It's not easy to grasp some of these concepts and put shapes
and forms around then, but that's what the Qabalah offers—

a way of putting even the most abstract ideas into action and refining them until they become tangible and workable.

Allow yourself to continue dreaming today. Take some time out, be gentle on yourself, and appreciate the beauty of the world in which you live. Connect with the elements within as well as those you can see, and spend time spoiling yourself. Perhaps you don't do that often enough? Love is always the answer, no matter the question, but love begins and ends with you.

During your "me" day remember to consolidate your experiences over the last three days.

Consolidation

Begin by asking yourself some questions. Let your intuition flow, and think about the planets, Sephiroth, Tarot cards, images, and visualizations you have recently encountered.

- Ask yourself again what your dream, your goal is.

- Looking at each Sephira, how has it reflected in your life?

- Binah—what does understanding mean to you? Where can you find inner silence?

- Chokmah—do you act on those flashes of inspiration? What are you inspired to do?

- Kether—can you be content with nothing? Why do you get attached to material things that you know won't bring you happiness?

- If you know your chart, look at Saturn, Uranus, and Neptune. What information do they give you?

- Put the following cards on a table in their relevant positions: the Empress horizontally; the Magician/Magus at a 45-degree angle on the left; the Fool at a 45-degree angel on the right.

- Look at the cards, analyze them, and think about how they might work with the Sephira and in your life.

Visualization: The Wheel of the Zodiac

Now it's time for your penultimate visualization of these 21 days.

Before you begin, set up for the visualization as you did previously. Then after lighting your candle, as before begin breathing in a 4-2-4-2 pattern: breathe in, nice and deep, for four seconds. Hold it for two, breathe out for four seconds, then hold it for two again. Repeat a few times, each time relaxing more and more.

Close your eyes and make your way into your forest. When you arrive at the clearing, enter the Tree to Malkuth.

Sandalphon is waiting for you. He guides you to the pillars and you stand in front of them: ebony on your left, ivory on your right. As you face the pillars, you see a curtain with a thin veil hanging from the center.

Sandalphon asks you to watch, to look through the veil. The violet light of Yesod gives way to the green of Netzach, and fading in now is the golden-yellow light of Tiphareth. As that wanes, the ruby-red of Geburah appears, slowly changing into the sapphire blue of Chesed.

Now you hear the ocean. Imagine a woman standing on a cliff edge, looking out to sea. She is waiting for a loved one to return. Can you glimpse Tzaphkiel—perhaps the dark shadow of his armor?

As the vision of Binah fades, it is replaced with a view of space— outer space; a star-lit sky. Suddenly out of nowhere comes a spinning zodiac wheel. Which sign lights up for you? (It may not be your own Sun sign.) Ratziel stands on the wheel in the sign of Aquarius, sparking with electricity, energy constantly in movement. Now that image fades and you are left with a white veil.

Just when you think the visualization is drawing to a close, you catch a glimpse of… what was that? There it is again—maybe it was your imagination? You can't explain it; you can't touch it;

nothing is there… or is it? Perhaps it's Metatron, waiting for you to be crowned as ruler of your own kingdom?

When you're ready, let that image fade and bring yourself back to Malkuth. Sandalphon guides you back to the altar. Thank him and then make your way out of the temple and into the clearing, then back into the forest.

Now, when you are ready, bring your awareness back into the room you're in. Slowly open your eyes, and wiggle your fingers and toes. As before, if you wish you can now make yourself refreshments.

Recording Your Journey

Now, as you did with the previous visualizations, take out your journal and write down your experience. Make notes about what you saw, felt, thought.

You have built the Tree in your mind, on your astral body, in the spiritual worlds, and in the pages of your journal. It will now be a part of you for ever and even if you choose not to go any further, you will always have these images and references with you.

For the rest of today allow yourself to contemplate ways of making your Tree your own. Perhaps you could draw a bigger one for your wall; maybe you wish to revisit each Sephira again, this time taking longer to experience them. And, of course, you still need to explore all those Tarot paths.

Tomorrow you're going to revisit Malkuth, but this time it's about increasing the power and learning a technique to help you get more from each Sephira and path, should you choose to go to them all again, more slowly this time. Just as you probably thought you were coming to the end of the journey, you are going to realize that it is a new beginning, as is so often the case with spiritual work.

Until tomorrow, fellow traveler.

DAY 21

Malkuth Revisited

"The meaning of life is not to be discovered only after death in some hidden, mysterious realm; on the contrary, it can be found by eating the succulent fruit of the Tree of Life and by living in the here and now as fully and creatively as we can."

PAUL KURTZ

Pick an oracle or Tarot card, and in your journal write down what card it is and what it means.

Over the last 20 days, we have learned some very useful visualizations. Today we are going to revisit Malkuth and cover a full path-working.

Make an Altar

To help you make the most of the your path-workings and to give you a focal point, it's a good idea to set up an altar and place items of relevance on it. For working with Malkuth, you might put fresh fruit, ivy leaves, flowers and herbs—symbols of the Earth and all its beauty—on your altar.

Always place a candle in the center. This can also acts as the candle for the East and Air. Then add three more candles for the South, the West, and the North, which represent Fire, Water, and Earth. Light them in a clockwise fashion and when you have finished working, allow time to let them burn out safely. You can put them all on a tray for this purpose; you don't have to leave them where they are. Avoid putting them out, if you can.

Place an icon or symbol on your altar that speaks to you of the work you're doing—something like a picture or statue of an earth goddess, or perhaps a blue crystal bowl with your central candle in it, just as you would see in Malkuth.

Burn incense that's relevant to the path you're working on, and give yourself time to let the energy build. When I do a path-working I make an appointment with myself. I sit down and ask for the spiritual worlds to assist me at X o'clock and

I am always, without fail, ready to start at that time. When I begin I ring a bell with reverence, as the sound of a bell can be heard in the astral worlds. (But remember, you are requesting spiritual beings to assist you, not summoning the butler!)

I set up at least half an hour before I'm due to start, to allow time for the energy to build up. To maintain it once the candles are lit and the incense is burning, I use music that's appropriate to the task in hand.

I recommend that you have a shower and put on clean, fresh clothing before you start. If you can, keep some comfortable clothing only for path-working.

A word of caution—always check your Moon calendar before doing a path-working. If there is a new Moon, don't do any path-workings three days prior to it, as this is the period of the dark Moon and is not conducive to this sort of work.

Before you begin, remember to set up as you did previously for visualizations. Then after lighting your candle, as before begin breathing in a 4–2–4–2 pattern: breathe in, nice and deep, for four seconds. Hold it for two, breathe out for four seconds, then hold it for two again. Repeat a few times, each time relaxing more and more.

We are going to start with the Qabalistic Cross—but with a difference. This time, we're bringing in the archangels.

- Taking a deep breath, raise and extend your arms up and out to your sides as if you were making a cross. Visualize four tall, robed, and hooded figures surrounding you, each standing facing a different direction.

- Say: "Before me RAPHAEL, Behind me GABRIEL, to my right hand MICHAEL, to my left hand URIEL. Around me burn the pentagrams and behind me shines the six-rayed star of pure white brilliance." (Uriel is the Archangel of the Earth; Sandalphon is the Archangel of Humanity.)

Opposite is a diagram showing all the Archangels in their Sephiroth on the Tree of Life.

You can take this to a higher level, but that is beyond the remit of this book. For now this will increase the energy to help you get a better experience and more clarity during your visualization.

So take your time, make your appointment, set up your room, decorate it, and light your candles. Now we're going to do the Malkuth visualization again.

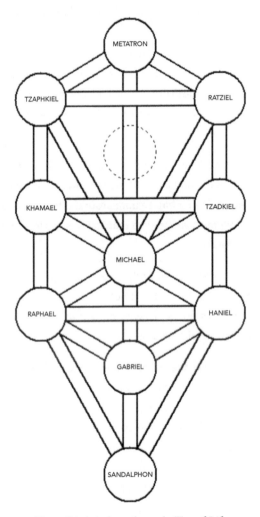

Figure 21.1 Archangels on the Tree of Life

Visualization:
The Temple of Malkuth Revisited

See yourself in a forest. Build it around you and make it as real as you can. See it, feel it, hear it, and smell it. Walk along the path and if an animal comes your way, acknowledge it. This is another symbol—an aspect of yourself or perhaps a power animal just for you.

Follow the path to a clearing, a well-kept place with flower borders and a beautiful lawn. At the far end you see a giant oak tree. It's magnificent! It has an aura around it that sparkles in the light and it seems to vibrate in a magical way. It's the Tree of Life. Stop and feel its magic.

In its base is a great oak door that opens as you approach. Step inside. At first you notice the smell of damp earth and wood. Then the aroma of herbs fills your nostrils as you move into this space—the Temple of Malkuth.

You look down and see herbs strewn across a black-and-white tiled floor. They release their fragrance as you walk over them. Your eyes become accustomed to the light and you begin to peer around you. The walls are covered in oak and ahead of you there is a double-cubed altar, with one cube of ebony and one of ivory. On the altar there is a simple white cloth with a blue crystal bowl set upon it. In the bowl burns a flame. Ahead of the altar are two pillars, one of ebony and one of ivory. Behind them are three great doors.

On the eastern wall above the three great doors is a circular stained-glass window featuring the face of a man, which represents Aquarius and the symbol for Air. To your right and in the south there is another window, showing a lion rampant (a lion in an upright position, as seen on the Scottish flag). This is the symbol for Leo and Fire. Behind you in the west, the window depicts an eagle flying into a golden sun—the symbol for Scorpio and Water. And to your left, in the north, the window shows a black bull in a field of poppies, the symbol for Taurus and Earth.

Stand in the center of the temple, and await the presence of Archangel Sandalphon. As he appears the atmosphere changes. This humble and magnificent being comes toward you, his robe the colors of earth: red, olive, and brown. These robes seem to weigh him down for he is the Archangel of Humanity, charged with our care. He smiles and welcomes you, and asks you to face the eastern wall. He then places his hand on your shoulder or head in a blessing.

This time he leaves you to look around the temple, to see what else you can glean, and to enjoy your new clarity.

When you're ready, see Sandalphon come toward you. He asks you what you wish to manifest on Earth. He reminds you that your own Tree is now taking root and is ready to bear you fruit.

When you're ready, it's time to leave. Let Sandalphon lead you to the door and back into the clearing. You (and your animal, if you've seen one) go back into the forest. You say farewell to the animal and let the forest fade as you bring yourself back into the here and now.

Slowly open your eyes, and wiggle your fingers and your toes. If you wish, you can now get up and make yourself refreshments.

Recording Your Journey

"A dream is your creative vision for your life in the future. You must break out of your current comfort zone and become comfortable with the unfamiliar and the unknown."

Denis Waitley

Once you're refreshed, get out your journal and fill it with even more understanding and wisdom from your return visit to Malkuth.

Remember, this method is about helping you through life, it's not just learned once then forgotten. Use it every day, in the here and now, as well as once in a while to gain a deeper understanding of what's going on.

Also make sure you use it *your* way. For example, if you have a problem with relationships, go into Netzach and look around, temper your thoughts, or listen to your soul. Then visit Hod or Tiphareth, find where you are, and work out how to get to where you want to be.

Afterword

The Qabalah is a study that will take you on many journeys. You will meet new spiritual guides, view the world in different ways, and start to question what you may have thought of as "normal" for years.

Questioning is a gift that humanity has been given in order for us to find our way back to our Source, so ask away! The Qabalah will bring you some answers, but it will also always leave you with yet another question. This is the process that truly brings growth to your personality, your soul, and ultimately brings you back to your spirit.

This book is but a small taste, the *hors d'oeuvre* before the banquet, so I hope you enjoy it and, when you're ready, move on to explore the many more treats that the Qabalah has to offer.

David Wells

Further Resources

There are many resources and teaching courses available, but as with all these things, just be sure you listen to your intuition. If something doesn't feel right, ask questions—and if you're not happy with the answers, be prepared to walk away and look elsewhere.

Also by David Wells:

The Tree of Life Oracle (2023)

Qabalah Made Easy (2021)

About the Author

David Wells is an outstanding astrologer, past life therapist, author, teacher and presenter whose unique sense of humor and vibrant personality captivates audiences far and wide. With successful television appearances on *Your Stars, Jane Goldman Investigates, Big Brother, Fame Academy, RI:SE, GMTV, Heaven on Earth* and *Most Haunted,* David is a popular household name within the paranormal genre. He was also a columnist with *Now* and *Fate and Fortune,* and the astrologer for Scotland's *Daily Record* and for *Spirit and Destiny* magazine.

David is contacted on a weekly basis by thousands of people who seek his expert guidance. David was born in Kelloholm in Scotland. The turning point in his life came in 1992 when he was hospitalized with severe pneumonia. He remembers being aware of walking down a hospital corridor whilst knowing that his physical body was still in a bed on the ward. Following training in a mystery school, David's abilities began to develop at an alarming rate. He studied astrology to ground his abilities, and searched for meaningful ways to discover more about himself and to fulfil his life purpose. It has been a long road from catering manager to spiritual teacher, and along the way David has discovered personal strengths and faced many weaknesses, or as he puts it, 'admitted to them!' His philosophy is this: never be so heavenly minded that you are of no earthly use! Combine the two: live every day with your eyes and heart wide open and you will travel the road without falling over the obstacles.

www.davidwells.co.uk

CONNECT WITH
HAY HOUSE
ONLINE

 hayhouse.co.uk   **f** @hayhouse

 @hayhouseuk   🐦 @hayhouseuk

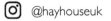 @hayhouseuk    @hayhouseuk

Find out all about our latest books & card decks • Be the first to know about exclusive discounts • Interact with our authors in live broadcasts • Celebrate the cycle of the seasons with us • Watch free videos from your favourite authors • Connect with like-minded souls

'The gateways to wisdom and knowledge are always open.'

Louise Hay